WITHIN THESE STREETS

Also published by Prison Book Ministries Ltd:

Killing Time—The nightmare of an innocent man branded a killer, by Noel Fellowes

WITHIN THESE STREETS

The true story of a young man's survival in life's minefield

Jimmy Rice
with Noel Fellowes

Prison Book Ministries Ltd

Published in the United Kingdom by:
Prison Book Ministries Ltd, PO Box 40
Hinckley, Leicestershire LE10 3LX

Copyright © 1993 Jimmy Rice & Noel Fellowes
First published by Prison Book Ministries Ltd July 1993

All rights reserved.
No part of this publication may be reproduced or transmitted, in any form or by any means, electronic or mechanical, including photocopy, recording or any information storage and retrieval system, without permission in writing from the publisher.

Edited, designed and typeset in the United Kingdom by:
Life Skills Training Services, 163 Clifton Road
Rugby, Warwickshire CV21 3QN

Printed in Russia

Contents

Foreword by Noel Fellowes ... 7
1 Running wild ... 9
2 Banged up ... 24
3 Struggle for freedom ... 33
4 Breaking-point ... 44
5 Rescued ... 57
6 A daily choice ... 72
7 Rocky road to love ... 82
8 Joanne ... 91
9 Roller coaster living ... 102
10 Growing pains ... 117
11 Fighting for life ... 128
12 Breaking through ... 135
13 Entering a new season ... 148

Dedication

This books is dedicated to my wife and best friend, Joanne, as well as my three daughters: Sarah-Jane, Billie Jean and Ruby Joy

Foreword

Why do so many young people go off the rails? Why do they so easily enter a life of crime and violence? We in society are confused when we encounter crime. It seems so senseless and purposeless. It unsettles and often frightens us.

Jimmy Rice was one such young person who seemed destined to spend much of his life behind bars.

In my experience of working with prisoners and ex-prisoners, there's often a hidden story lurking behind the macho image and external show of self-confidence. It's one of pain, suffering, rejection, violence and abuse. It's the result of wrong role models and belief systems. Many have been born into social deprivation and breast fed on it.

Jimmy, like so many young people, found himself in the battlefield of life, one in which no one had taught him the rules of engagement or survival. He lived on the streets and in areas where social deprivation was at its worst. His neighbours were drunks, drug addicts, pushers, prostitutes and street gang members.

He lived in the fast lane, courted popularity, became part of the action—king of the concrete jungle with a name and reputation to uphold.

Then he pressed the self-destruct button. A deadly cocktail of drugs, alcohol and violence helped to express his frustration and anger at a system that made no room for understanding his inner pain, anxiety and longing for love, security and fulfilment.

Over a number of years Jimmy and I have carved out a great friendship. It's been a long, painful process as we've worked at the coalface of each other's lives and experiences. But it's a friendship earthed in truth, reality and vulnerability. This is the only way it could work for us as we'd travelled down similar paths in life —paths of pain, suffering and injustice.

It's a great privilege to have such a friend as Jimmy and to have worked so closely with him in writing this book. Not only is his story true, but he's the genuine article. Jimmy isn't a man who lives in the past or wallows in it. You literally have to drag the past out of him.

In my opinion, he's earned the right to share the intimate details of his life and experience, to help unlock other lives that have been bruised or broken. And his story can be an effective tool for preventing other young people ever starting in a life of crime.

In this book you'll enter the trauma and nightmares of the tragic reality of a young man trying to survive in a world full of destruction and dashed dreams. You'll read of the endless battles he encounters as he finally comes to terms with hope, reconciliation and purpose in his long, painful search for truth and reality.

As you enter the pages of Jimmy's life you'll find pages of your own. As you encounter his victories over adversity, you'll find answers for your own.

Just like Jimmy, you can *overcome!*

Noel Fellowes
July 1993

1
Running wild

I was dragged out of sleep, a hand tightly gripping my collar, bulging eyes staring close and a hammer raised to strike.

I just hoped that within a split second he'd recognise me.

'James! What are you doing here?' asked Uncle Jack, loosening his grip.

'I've run away,' came the answer, fright squirting the truth straight out of my mouth.

'Come on, lad,' said Jack, lumbering his thick frame across the backyard of his terraced house.

I gathered my things to follow, wondering what his reaction might be. Jack had always been my favourite uncle, but running away might be stretching things a bit too far.

I'd arrived home late the previous night to find my dad's house locked and in darkness. Dreading a telling off, I'd knocked tentatively, almost hoping not to be heard. After four attempts I remembered he was on sleeping pills following a recent car crash and was unlikely to hear a thing.

I stood on the doorstep, the cold reminding me of the long night ahead. Anger and self-pity stirred inside.

My mind wandered back over recent years leading up to my parents' separation. After starting secondary school at age 11, my behaviour, which had always been boisterous, deteriorated badly. Academic progress was stifled by my rebellion and my constant desire to argue. I was more interested in pursuing a name for myself, showing off to the girls and playing football.

It was easy to get hold of strong drink; I loved the wild abandon it gave me. But the aggression it sparked made my friends increasingly wary of me at school. I reached the point where I was barred from class and made to work in isolation.

My parents split up. My mother took me, along with my

younger sister and brother, to live by the Liverpool docks on the Mersey.

Moving to a different area was hard for us all. My new school was scruffy and less disciplined than the previous one, but at least I was able to flex my unsettled personality.

While Mother struggled with social security problems, along with all the emotional upheaval of the move, I got my kicks out on the streets. With Dad out of the way I skipped school, staying out late and mixing with a rough bunch.

I was involved in a drunken disturbance one evening and arrested by the police. I was still aged 13 and classed as a juvenile, so a guardian was needed to collect me. News that Dad was coming rather than Mother sobered me up in double-quick time. I sat in the cell anxiously awaiting the confrontation. But to my surprise he reacted calmly and simply asked during the drive home, 'Want a ciggie, son?'

It felt weird smoking in front of him, but a better atmosphere developed between us. Later he asked me to move back to live with him. My acceptance came more out of politeness than desire; it was confusing to know what I really wanted.

Just two weeks later I stood on the doorstep, kicking my heels in the cold.

It suited me to believe he'd locked me out deliberately, offering a convenient excuse to cut loose and run away. This little tale of rejection would deflect the blame on to Dad nicely while drumming up sympathy for me. I liked a bit of sympathy.

As I crept round the back of the house to break in and collect some things, my emotions rocked on a seesaw between excitement and fear. Entering an upstairs window proved extremely difficult, but once inside another dilemma faced me. There before me was my old bed; I need only to climb in and sleep, putting an end to this quandary.

The light of common sense laid bare my self-delusion, weakening my resolve to go. But quickly, aggressively, I suppressed the feelings, snatched up a few belongings and disappeared.

The full impact of my actions hit me as I walked along those long, empty roads. Many anguished tears fell as the pain of separation gripped me in a way I'd never expected.

'What have I done?' I asked myself again and again.

The light of new hope kept my legs walking despite the intrusion of a thousand burning thoughts. After three hours I stood outside my destination. Uncle Jack had a disused car inside the lockup at the end of his backyard. I could rest there for a while and be gone before he got up.

Breaking in was easy but, once inside, I found it intolerably cold, smelly and uncomfortable. Sleep seemed impossible but somehow, shivering and tired, I dropped off while sitting up.

Smelling fusty like the old car, I now sat feeling miserable in front of a heater in the back room. Uncle Jack talked through the open door of the kitchen while cooking chips for breakfast. Jack thought chips were a great idea and set to work peeling spuds while I, hardly feeling able to refuse, dreaded their arrival.

Uncle Jack lived alone after years of illness. Periods in hospital had followed peculiar incidents, the details of which were kept from 'little ears'. 'Your Uncle Jack's not well, son,' was the family line.

During our conversation my ears pricked up when I heard, 'I'll get you a job on the site with me, lad.'

'Thanks, Uncle Jack,' I replied. I was playing it cool but, inside, my heart leapt at this sudden upturn in fortune. Now I had a place to hide, a job—and I wasn't being packed off home as expected. It wasn't the glittering start I'd dreamed of, but it'd serve to make the family realise I wasn't about to come crying home.

The heater drew out my tiredness, producing a string of yawns. With my eyes red and watery, the greasy chips arrived accompanied by a bottle of brown sauce. I struggled through enough to satisfy Jack then, with my immediate worries over, fell asleep.

The following day Jack had me up early, running bleary-eyed through the estate for a bus. Despite my appearing much older than 14 and clearly dressed for work, Uncle Jack paid my half fare. The driver complied under his forthright manner while I sat looking out of the window, embarrassed.

When we arrived on site I was appointed can-lad (tea-maker) by the boss, whose grumpy attitude flattened any enthusiasm. Setting about my duties, I reflected on the rude awakening my romantic idea of running away had received.

But it was at night that I had my fun, hanging out with the gang in the shopping precinct and town centre. Staying out late and having a good time with them was the main attraction for leaving home. Many of the kids stayed off school and wandered the streets almost every day. Others showed up mostly at night to see what was happening.

The shopping precinct was at the hub of gang activity in our area. The estate was called 'Westminster' and the gang the 'Wezzie Mob'. The store windows were boarded up each night, providing further space for graffiti to be sprayed.

A seedy nightclub owned by an American sat in the middle of the shopping precinct. It was a miracle he kept his licence with all the fights that took place both inside and out. The prostitutes, who brought sailors from the docks, gave us cigarettes on the way in. We slunk around, sometimes picking up valuables that were dropped during scuffles or trying to part a drunk with his money.

The precinct was a colourful place where anything could happen. I'd envied those whose poor upbringing allowed a type of behaviour I'd never been permitted. I wanted to be associated with their rough identity and share the wild fruits of their undisciplined lives. Despite equipping myself with an excuse for running away and willingly joining in their late-night escapades, this was a rough district where acceptance wasn't guaranteed.

One night at a local disco I danced with a girl I fancied called Donna. Unfortunately, she was going out with Jonah, a lad I didn't know.

Donna liked me and confessed she wanted to get rid of Jonah. 'He's always with his stupid mates and never bothers with me.'

Later, everybody spilled out on to the precinct and were joined by others who hung around the nearby streets. The atmosphere buzzed with shouts, whistles, smoke, singing and laughter.

Donna's friend tugged my sleeve. 'Jonah's here with his mates. You'd better clear off in case he starts.'

I didn't like to be frightened away, but the warmth previously enjoyed as part of the crowd had now become punctuated by steely looks. Feeling unsure, I drew heavily on my cigarette before stepping aside to leave.

My head exploded and the world turned sideways as I felt myself being dragged across the pavement by my hair. The crowd jostled for position amid screams as—in sheer panic—I grappled furiously for a hold on my attacker.

We wrestled, kicked and clashed heads until I broke Jonah's grip, knocked him to the ground, jumped on top and began punching.

A figure darted forward to kick me, followed by others, until I was sprawled out across the floor, unconscious. Another scuffle broke out as somebody tried to help, while the girls screamed and punched those who'd kicked me.

I regained consciousness leaning against the wall of a nearby back alley. An echoing voice became that of a girl holding me up. She'd apparently helped me stagger away as the police arrived. She gave me a cigarette and related what had happened. It was clear that I'd beaten Jonah before the attack by his mates.

Instead of seeking revenge, I looked forward to the increased street cred this fight was sure to bring me.

After just two weeks at work I was laid off, which satisfied my real desire to be out on the streets with my mates. We wandered around causing aggro, stealing, fighting, vandalising, tattooing each other and generally causing a rumpus wherever we went.

Still sleeping at Uncle Jack's, I arrived home late one night to find him in a state of anxiety.

'That stupid idiot over the back is giving me aggro,' he said heatedly.

'Who?' I asked.

'That bald-headed bloke in the side street. We're going to sort him out good style,' he went on.

I couldn't understand what had caused the problem and suspected there may be no real reason at all. But the turmoil hidden inside him was there to be seen in his eyes.

In the early hours of the morning he and I crept along the street and hammered six-inch nails into all four tyres on the man's van.

During the weeks that followed I drifted away from Jack's, preferring instead to stay with the crowd I was now meeting in the pubs. These older ones weren't into hanging round street corners waiting for the next gang fight. They liked to drink in comfort, buy good drugs, waltz in and out of clubs and breeze through life.

Occasionally they ended up skint, but information would soon filter through about a lucrative job to pull off. It was common to pay store detectives to disappear for five minutes while a group carried off expensive equipment.

During this time I met up with Denny, an old school friend. He was fascinated by all I'd been getting up to since hitting the streets. The gang at the precinct made him welcome, sharing ciggies, money and drink each night before he caught his bus home. Denny couldn't get served in the pub so we had to sneak him in and keep him hidden.

After a few weeks I got tired of him. Having to cater for the obstacle of his young looks was a hindrance to the big plans I had for myself. So I began avoiding him, letting him wander around alone until finally he stopped coming. It hurt my feelings, but I'd soon forget him just like I'd done with my family.

Following a few close shaves with the police, I was eventually arrested. This time they called my mother. My head dropped in dismay, knowing the further grief I was bringing on her.

In the taxi driving home, my mother tried through her own tears to cheer me. But I remained impassive, brushing off any attempt by her even to touch me. I no longer believed I had any right to her love.

'Why can't you just forget me like I forget you?' I demanded. 'Just leave me alone. I'm no good for you any more.'

My painful words and actions were intended to push her to the brink, to force her to reject me so we could both be free.

'You'll have your own kids one day. Then you'll understand,' she said, repeating a phrase I'd heard many times before.

While waiting for my summons to court I was told I had to live at home and start a new school. I enjoyed some aspects of home life but found conflicts hard to handle. Soon I ran off again.

This began a pattern of events that repeated themselves many times over subsequent years. I went to a number of schools while living with a succession of relatives after various arrests. Despite my growing toughness, my over-sensitivity at home began shaping my behaviour out on the streets. I moved around, drifting from one gang to another and one girl to another, never wanting to commit myself to anybody.

Things came to a head one evening when, having taken a cocktail of drink and drugs, I arrived home to give mouthfuls of screaming abuse to everybody. They couldn't control me so they called the police.

I left calmly and stood chatting with the police a few doors along the street.

'Come on, sunshine, we don't want to arrest you. You've just had a little argument, that's all. Now, why don't you go back, say you're sorry and that'll be that.'

'OK, I will,' I said. 'Thanks.'

As they climbed back in I smashed a rock on to their car and stood laughing. The police and I fought all the way to the cells, where I was locked up for the night. This time they had me up before the magistrates within days.

My dad went with me to the court, where we sat in a tall, shiny hall waiting to be called. People stood in small murmuring groups wearing ill-fitting suits, looking worried. Through the haze of cigarette smoke and clicking footsteps on the marble floor I heard a man calling: 'James Rice? Do we have a James Rice?'

Dad and I stood.

'This must be it, then,' said Dad.

A ruddy-faced man in a black gown approached, carrying a bundle of papers. 'Are you James Rice?' he barked for all to hear.

'Yes, I am.'

'Then you'd better take these.' He leafed off court charges into my hands one after the other. 'Rice, Rice, Rice, Rice, Rice . . . .'

I quickly glanced through, recognising each incident with a shudder. 'Oh, hell,' I thought.

Without having time to digest these fresh crimes, we were called in.

With the opening formalities over, the prosecutor began reading out the charges. Hearing them presented in such stark terms was like being undressed in public. I became painfully aware of my dad standing there, hearing all this just a few metres away.

What would the magistrates think of this wild, drunken, violent account of me rolled out before them? I dreaded to think. My plea of guilty was the signal for much flapping in outrage from the magistrates. Things looked bad.

After my dad spoke a few words they softened down. But then up rose the clerk, who pecked away at the bench with stern advice in hushed tones.

The fat magistrate in the middle motioned for quiet, turned to me and said: 'Young man, there has to be recompense for your behaviour.'

I held my breath, listening, trying to look as innocent as possible.

'We find no alternative but to sentence you to three months in a detention centre.'

My legs turned to jelly as I was taken down the steps into the cells. Three months is nothing if you say it quickly, yet the weight of it was suddenly killing me.

'What a whimp I really am!' I thought.

My pockets were emptied, forms signed and handcuffs placed on my wrists ready for a four-hour trip into the unknown. Looking out of the windows as we sped along I wished I was somebody else. I hated my life.

The safe haven of the journey ended all too soon as we pulled up outside two large brown gates in the countryside. The place seemed unnaturally quiet and clean as I was led through a series of locked doors to the reception area.

An officer appeared and, with a friendly smile, asked my name.
'Jimmy,' was the simple reply.

Smack! My head spun. He'd cracked me around the face hard. 'You call me "sir". Don't ever forget it.'

I wouldn't!

The police looked embarrassed while signing me over into detention centre custody.

I was gripped with fear, feeling vulnerable in the hands of my captors. 'Anything could happen to me here,' I thought.

By keeping my mouth shut, I survived the reception procedure without much fuss. As others were brought in I was locked in a tiny cell to wait. My mind wandered back to my old school where even now my class would be doing physical education or lessons. My heart retched in anguish. Why couldn't I have stuck at school and lived a simple life? It all seemed so far away now.

Later, I was unlocked and led with four other newcomers to a large dining room filled with lads who sat staring as we were allocated seats. I took an instant dislike to the one who sat opposite me, probing me with questions: 'Where're you from? How long you doing?'

I was too deep within myself to be bothered giving an answer. I merely murmured, 'I don't have to answer you, so shut it.'

Long before dark we were locked up for the night. As newcomers we'd have to sleep alone in tiny cells for a week before moving into a dormitory.

As the door locked shut, the walls seemed to close in to suffocate me. My freedom was gone. I had nothing. The pain was too much to bear—and this was only the first night.

I wanted to cry out but I held everything inside. I began thinking back again to happier days, this time to my sister and brother, whose innocence ensured the warm embrace of family life. 'Why've I gone this way? Why can't I accept a simple life?'

It was a long, hot night, filled with unhappy thoughts and dread of the morning.

The next day turned out to be equally eventful, beginning with a visit to the governor. He told me I'd have to serve only six weeks of my sentence, which was great news.

After this, I was set to work scrubbing floors on hands and knees until late afternoon. No talking or smoking was allowed, and this made the day drag on for ever.

Before supper we were taken to the canteen (prison shop) to be given advance pay. Nobody was allowed cash, but we were given goodies to the value of our earnings. We lined up behind another work party while our escort officer disappeared for a chat with somebody.

A lad from the party ahead turned to me and asked, 'How long you in for, dickhead?'

I couldn't believe my ears. 'You what?' I answered angrily.

'Oh, he's getting upset now,' he laughed to his friend.

Somehow this lad seemed to think there was no danger in what he was saying. I stepped forward and threw him against the wall, which he bounced off on to the floor.

At that moment the officer returned. 'Who did that?' he asked.

'I did, sir, he . . . .'

But he backed off to press a button without listening. The stupid lad stayed on the floor as a group of officers arrived almost immediately to grab me. They dragged me down to the punishment block and locked me in a cell alone.

An hour later I was brought out and marched into a room to face the governor. They stood me on a slippery mat to prevent me attacking anybody, while two officers stood in front staring at me.

A round-looking officer in a fancy hat barked: 'Rice, you are accused of assaulting prisoner Baker. Do you plead guilty or not guilty?'

I couldn't believe this. It was like a courtroom or court martial. 'Well, it wasn't just . . . .'

He cut me off. 'Guilty or not guilty?' he pressed.

'Well . . . .'

This time his face turned red and he slobbered as he shouted. *'Did you do it or not?'*

'Yes, sir.'

The governor scribbled as the round one whispered.

Then: 'Rice, you've come here with a bad record. We won't accept your violent behaviour. You'll spend seven days in the punishment block, lose three weeks' pay and three days' remission. Do you understand?'

I didn't, but said, 'Yes, sir,' and was quick-marched out to be slammed into the bare cell again.

The punishment block was much tougher than the rest of the place. It was a mixture of painful isolation, gruelling work and punishing workouts in the gym. My physical strength and ability with a ball helped me get on with the gym staff, but didn't excuse me from some of the nasty games. I was often placed in a circle in the middle of the hall while two lads at a time were sent in to fight me out of it.

Many made only feeble attempts. Others, goaded on by the staff, really had a go. I bounced them all out every time, much to the amusement of the punishment block officer.

My first good feelings came when I was released from 'the block' back into cubicles. Everything seemed so relaxed and easy compared to the regime I'd just come from.

It was about this time that I noticed how young many of the lads seemed, despite our all being about the same age. There were some bad ones, but I couldn't imagine how others had ever reached a detention centre. Some looked permanently bewildered and cried at night.

A lad called Ginger, who spoke like a posh schoolboy, was truly out of place. He'd giggle nervously at those who tried to bully him, which infuriated them. When an officer bawled at him one day for not scrubbing a floor properly, he laughingly said, 'Oh, come on,' as if addressing a loving grandad. The officer went berserk, kicked Ginger's bucket all over the floor and made him scrub everything again.

Eventually I was moved into a dormitory, which I shared with 20 other lads. It was like a hospital ward without the frills. Ginger approached as I unrolled my kit. 'You'll have to do a dorm run tonight, Ricey. Everybody has to.'

'What's a dorm run?' I asked without looking up.

'You have to climb over one bed, then under the next, all the way round the dorm, while everybody hits you with pillowcases filled with boots and shoes.'

'And who's going to get me to do that?' I asked.

'Makin,' he said. 'He's the cock of the dorm.'

As the room filled with lads, Ginger pointed Makin out.

After shooting him a quick glance I said, 'He can do mine for me.'

Ginger disappeared looking excited while I sat quietly on my bed. Soon enough, Makin approached.

'You're new, then? You'll have to do a dorm run, you know.'

He didn't order me like he might some of the others—more a request.

'*You* can do mine, pal,' I said.

'What?' he asked, looking bemused.

'You can do mine,' I said again, this time standing up and staring. 'I'm not doing any dorm run, so beat it. Go on.'

He backed off quickly, trying to limit the damage to his reputation, knowing that his personal domination over the place was over.

The lads soon learnt that I was no newcomer but had been kept in the punishment block and cubicles following a 'fight'. I paid no interest in pushing anybody around. I simply wanted to get through my sentence the easiest way possible.

Over the following weeks the lads who'd previously been bullied by Makin came out of their shells and began giving him plenty of stick.

Slaphead, a skinhead with a cross tattooed on his forehead and who was as thick as two short planks, crept up to his bed late at night and bit his finger as hard as he could. Makin nearly screamed the place down, clasping his hand in pain while Slaphead stood looking on with staring eyes and an insane grin.

Following the harsh regime of each day, the period between supper and sleep was often filled with the excited chatter of relief. Some read books or wrote home. Others curled up in bed, riddled with the pangs of homesickness, missing the comforts of the family life they'd so easily taken for granted.

Many had innocently become institutionalised after placements in a string of children's homes as a result of neglectful parenting. It was hard to imagine how they'd ever break their downhill spiral.

Release day itself was always tantalisingly elusive—so near yet so painfully far away. But, despite the frustration of it all, my last night soon arrived. I felt like a rich man. I was in possession of something everybody else craved for—imminent freedom.

As dawn broke I was up and packed before anybody had even stirred. The walk back down to the reception area was glorious. It was hard to keep from smiling all the way.

Putting my own clothes back on felt strange. They smelt musty, having been kept in a cardboard box. I was dropped off at the train station, where I joined a platform full of people heading for work.

The first cigarette made me feel sick. But it couldn't dampen my high spirits. While I never wanted to be put back inside, I looked forward to having some fun with my old pals again.

The emotional joy of release ran into a brick wall as I arrived at my new home, the YMCA. It was like a prison, with its long corridors, strangers, little rooms, locked doors, dining hall and plain food.

My social worker wasted no time in telling me that any misbehaviour within six weeks of release would result in my return to the detention centre. Fear of this kept me in line, but resentment built up at being trapped.

The family visited and were happy to accommodate my long-held desire to leave home.

'How are you, son? Everything all right?'

'Yeah, I'm fine, just fine,' I'd lie, keeping my pain hidden.

Really, I ached to come home, but couldn't express it. I was afraid that any cry from the heart would crumble my image and leave my identity in tatters.

I waited for the expiry of my six-week release conditions like a cat ready to pounce. Then I left without paying the rent.

Arriving back on familiar territory felt great. The gang at the precinct listened as I told them about detention centre. Others who'd also been inside laughed, remembering the fun they'd had in there and how easy it was. I wondered whether *they* were liars or *I'd* been too soft.

Many lads stole regularly, making plenty of money week after week, but that wasn't my style. I drifted around, joining the occasional raid to get money for drink, but then disappearing again. My aim in life was to avoid rules, regulations, work or anything that obstructed me. At night I walked the streets, then slept on the stairs of tower blocks, in sheds by the railway tracks or at parties I attended.

Many summer evenings were spent alone or with a girl down by the docks drinking whisky. In winter I moved into a house where young people hung out. Spray paint covered the inside walls. We burned the wardrobes to keep warm at night, and the curtains were kept permanently closed. People called in after the clubs to drink, take drugs and plan fights or robberies.

It was heaven to float around in a bubble of drink and drugs, untouched by the concerns of the world. We lived life in the fast lane with everything being done for kicks—clubbing, partying and stealing almost every day of every week. Scrapes with the law were customary. Twice I escaped a further custodial sentence by the skin of my teeth.

Yet my air of invincibility was challenged in court one day by the police, who tried hard to have me sent to Risley Remand Centre. This place had a notorious reputation for violence, misery, suicides and filth.

My grandad, who'd come to offer support, suddenly found the proceedings pivoting around his decision whether or not to stand bail. As he stood looking uncertain, with all eyes on him, my heart pounded.

'All right, I will,' he said at last.

Phew! I smiled with relief while Grandad looked on unhappily. My bail conditions were that I live at home, sign on at the police station every day and obey a 12-hour curfew.

I headed straight from court to the house I'd been living in to collect a few things. The gang there were amazed to see me, thinking I was sure to have been remanded in custody. Somebody produced a bottle of Bacardi rum which I started to drink by the glassful.

As we talked, one kid showed up who I suspected as being an informer, grassing on some friends of mine to the police. By including him in the conversation, I gave him no clue about my anger. When most of the bottle was gone, I quickly pounced. He screamed as I battered him with a fire poker. The others looked on terrified.

Suddenly, I collapsed on the floor, overcome by drink. The other lad, bleeding profusely, was helped to escape through a window, and they called an ambulance for me. I woke the following day in a hospital bed feeling like death warmed up. It's a terrible thing having a pipe shoved deep down your throat, then watching your guts pumped out into a glass vacuum-cleaner.

The police arrived to escort me back to court, having advised my grandad to withdraw his bail and save himself a £500 bill.

This time I floated through the proceedings and was taken away in a daze to the place I dreaded—Risley Remand Centre.

2
Banged up

The reception area was filled with noise. Prisoners were being herded through in various stages of undress. Those of us unfamiliar with procedures clenched our stomachs in anticipation while others with experience snorted on an air of nonchalance.

Whatever compassion the screws (prison officers) had originally brought to their jobs was now squeezed out, leaving a wall of cold indifference. Nobody cared. We were stripped of clothes, names and dignity as people looked on our vulnerability.

Once we were bathed and changed, they locked us in a large pen known as 'the cage'. Some sat in groups chatting while others perched uncomfortably alone, searching for space in which to stare.

We were taken along corridors to cells amid slamming doors, jangling keys, shouts and the mingled smell of food and urine. My cellmate, slumped on his bunk, didn't even look up as the door banged behind me.

I presumed mine to be the bottom bunk. There was no pillow. The mattress was filthy and torn. Graffiti covered the walls, the locker was broken and most of the windows were long since gone. The air was constantly filled with shouts between the facing cell blocks, with messages, singing, abuse and threats bouncing off the walls.

Our toilet for most of the day and all of each night was a plastic pot in the cell. Most people pissed into a jug or crapped on to a piece of sheet, then flung it out of the window. On hot days, the stench outside invaded everything and, when it rained, a sludge appeared. People volunteered for the 'crap shovelling party' because, after clearing up the mess, they were guaranteed a rare shower and change of clothes.

As I was unlocked one morning, two screws rushed past, dragging a lad covered in blood. I asked a cellmate what had happened.

'He's flipped, man, I tell you. He ate his own crap, drank his piss, then poured water all over himself and sat by the open window trying to catch pneumonia.'

'What about the blood?' I asked.

'He made me punch him in the nose until it bled, then laid across his bunk with his head hanging over, knocking it to keep the blood flowing.'

A dark circle of shiny congealed blood lay neatly on the floor like an evil chocolate pudding.

As we turned away laughing, I realised how little these incidents affected me. My hunger for enjoyment was increasingly satisfied at other people's expense or misfortune. It was a dog eat dog world in which we lapped up sick fun like snapping hyenas, giving reign to predatory instincts that chewed away at the conscience.

It was a disgraceful fact that half the inmates weren't convicted of any crime. A great many others would receive noncustodial sentences.

After three months, my case came before the crown court for sentencing. The joy had been knocked out of my life, and I hardly cared what would happen.

In the ancient cell beneath the court building I could almost feel the presence of those who, over the years, had passed through there before me. Their grief, pain, helplessness and fear lingered with mine.

The courtroom was grand, the judge all stern pomp. My eyes drifted to the public gallery as my life and charges were tossed about. A group of students sat in a bunch, one girl looking at me curiously. I envied the peace of her world and she may have envied the abandon of mine. I hoped she liked me.

Surprisingly, the judge took pity on me. He called on the probation service to offer me a scheme of some sort.

They refused, saying I'd be too hard to handle. The judge, expressing regret and some reluctance, sentenced me to Borstal (young offenders) training for between six months and two years.

Open Borstal was a minefield of petty rules run on similar lines to military training. The physical demands of training were impossibly hard and the cell inspections totally unachievable. One tiny crumb at the back of a drawer or a minuscule piece of fluff on the floor meant the cell was unfit for human habitation and had to be totally recleaned.

It was less strict than detention centre but cleaner and more humane then remand centre. They offered skills in building, welding and catering, along with classes in further education. I hated the place and refused them all, settling instead for more menial jobs where my thoughts could be my own.

'Why should I train for cheap, dirty jobs?' I reasoned. 'Life's got to mean more to me than *that.*'

I still held out the hope of an easy, work-free life away from the trappings of the rat race. We could expect to do just nine months of the sentence, but I lost two months' remission very quickly for absconding. A lad I knew had a friend who picked up a supply of milk early each morning from a small town 15 miles away. We planned to meet up with him, get a lift into Leeds and make a start from there.

We waited until the night-watchman had completed his hourly check, then ran off, climbing the perimeter fence and getting away across the fields. In our haste, running through pitch darkness, we got caught in barbed-wire, ripped our clothes in hedges, fell down holes and got covered in cuts and bruises. We kept going for hours until, by daybreak, we arrived at the edge of the town we were looking for.

As we climbed a river bank to cross the bridge into the high street, police arrived from everywhere and arrested us. This meant plenty more time in the punishment block thinking about what a stupid escapade it'd been.

Life in the block is a completely different world from the rest of an institution. The light is on 24 hours a day and no furniture is allowed. The books available to read are totally boring and nobody's allowed to speak.

I spent most of my time walking up and down humming,

whistling and getting more wound up with the terribly slow drag of time. A week in there turns your head inside out.

Back on the wing there was the usual bullying and intimidation. But I took up my customary position of not letting anybody push me around. Young men in prison are obsessed with pecking orders in terms of fighting, and they debate endlessly over who can beat who. They allotted me a high standing, which proved beneficial in some ways, but not in others.

There was a homosexual on our wing who was older than most of us. Nobody was too friendly with him through fear of being tarred with the same brush. He was playing table-tennis on the table behind the one I was using one evening. Our ball got cracked slightly, so when theirs came past after a winning shot I caught it and threw ours back without anybody noticing.

After a few shots he walked up, smiling. 'Come on, Ricey.'

'What?'

'You've nicked our ball. Come on.'

'Get lost. We're playing,' I said, and served.

'Oh, come on, Ricey. I know you've switched them.'

'Look, you'd better shut it!' I shouted.

We stood there, arms folded. I threw my bat down. 'You two, get out—now.'

The other two left. The guy stood, bat in hand, shaking.

'Put the bat down,' I demanded.

'What for?'

'Just put it down.'

After a pause he pointed the bat in my face and burst out: 'Rice, before you start, I want you to know you're an idiot, a dickhead. Why can't you use your *brains*, not your *fists?*'

He stood staring, shaking with sweat.

He was right and I knew it. I smiled in admiration while he looked confused.

'It's this stupid place,' I said at last. 'Let's just forget it.'

He couldn't believe it. The bell went for supper. I gave him a cigarette and we walked to the dining hall talking. The lads I'd chased out couldn't understand what was happening. His strength of honesty about his sexuality and courage in standing up against aggression left me feeling ashamed. This sharp reminder of my own cowardice stayed with me for weeks.

The slow drag of time was tortuous. I was irritated by those around me who constantly talked about cars and motorbikes like children looking at toys in a Christmas catalogue. Others turned their cells into shrines to girlfriends or pop heroes. Hostility simmered between people from different parts of the country, most of them being afraid of each other.

I settled into a routine, not wanting to lose any more remission. Sport was the one thing that kept me going. We played Rugby and soccer matches every week, interspersed with circuit training.

After eight months I was given five days' home leave. I was to spend my period in a probation hostel in Chester while suitable accommodation was being arranged for my full release. Home leave began at the train station, where two of us bought plenty of strong lager for the ride home.

The months in Borstal amounted to nothing as we gleefully drank the lager. Changing back into my denim clothes, I threw the new suit the Borstal had given me out of the window. We arrived in Manchester to change trains. While we were waiting for our connection, a guard approached and asked to see our tickets. Mine couldn't be found.

'We're on our way home from Borstal, mate. We've both got the same parole papers. Look,' I said.

He wasn't impressed and didn't like the look of us. 'You'd better come with me,' he said.

We followed him to a control room, where we were soon joined by the police. The two of us were locked up while they made enquiries. After a while we were taken into the rail chief's office where we stood like two scamps before his large, shiny desk.

'Now, then,' he said like Jimmy Savile. 'We've contacted your Borstal and they aren't happy about your drinking and loss of ticket. But they want you to continue with your home leave and they'll deal with matters when you return.'

I didn't like the sound of that.

'Which one of you's James Rice?'

'That's me,' I said.

'We're able to issue you with a . . . oh, God, no . . . .' He trailed off, looking at my companion with a grimace.

I was confused but followed the gaze and couldn't believe what I saw. My friend had stood there and wet himself all over the floor!

We were immediately sent from the room back to the police cells. After being issued with a new ticket and a strong caution for under-age drinking, they let me go.

I completed the journey alone, and was met by an irate lady probation officer who'd been kept waiting for hours. She showed me to the hostel, then disappeared as quickly as she could.

The place had a depressing air about it, being occupied by unemployed ex-prisoners who wore grey, beaten looks. After two unhappy days in this grubby place, thinking about the trouble I faced on my return, I cleared off back to my own area with the gang. I felt I had nothing more to lose and set about robbing, drinking, fighting and taking drugs.

The police actively pursued me, but I avoided them again and again. A month of this passed until I began to feel really down, wishing I had the stability to behave and return like anybody else. The other lads would be back now, getting nearer to the end of their sentences.

On the street my life was a source of intrigue and excitement. But, in truth, things were catching up on me. I envied those who could go home each night and whose futures didn't include the prospect of life behind bars like mine.

I was out with a girlfriend one night and asked her to marry me.

'I'm too young and you're too crazy,' she replied.

The following day she was furious to learn that I'd asked her friend, too!

Eventually the police burst in to arrest me at an apartment where I'd stayed too long. Despite the prospect of further sentencing by the courts, I admitted all my crimes, wanting somehow to wipe the slate clean and one day be truly free.

I was locked up at Walton Jail in Liverpool before being moved to the punishment block at Strangeways Prison in Manchester.

After an intensely depressing period in there, I was moved to Stoke Heath, a secure Borstal, and placed on a strict wing. In that place there was a good share of tough characters like me. They didn't bully anybody but resisted being pushed around. Our wing had a constantly bad atmosphere in which an uneasy standoff between the lads simmered.

A deep hatred began to fester as I tried to cope with the long wait for resentencing and an unknown release date. Unlike before, I didn't write to any girls. I wanted to avoid the prospect of being let down or hurt again.

My cell remained bare and undecorated. 'It's not my cell—it's your cell,' I'd say to the screws. 'Don't expect me to make a home of this dump. My home's outside, not in here.'

The screws sent me to the punishment block again and again for my aggressive attitude towards them. Those times were unspeakably painful, but my face remained rigid, giving away no trace of the hurt I felt inside.

When I reached crown court, the judge wanted to add three years to my sentence but relented, giving me Borstal again. I'd already served longer than anybody else, but I had to start again.

My job was coal shovelling. We were known as the Banjo Boys. It was the worst job in the Borstal, reserved for troublemakers. Each morning we sat on the coal stack watching the others file into the big workshops for the day. We filled large trucks with coal, pushed them to the coal stack, emptied them and started again—all day, rain or shine.

If one of us reported sick, the screw was obliged to take us all to the sick bay, which gave us a break.

We had a rota for reporting. 'Whose turn is it today?' we'd ask while shovelling.

'I'll have a go,' somebody'd say.

'Hey, boss, I've got a splitting headache. It's killing me.'

He'd radio through and we'd all traipse along slowly, a ragged bunch smoking and chatting. No matter what we complained of, the medic gave us two white tablets. Nobody knew what they were;

we just took them. We joked about an imaginary white tablet wagon dropping tonnes of them off for the 'white tablet shovelling party' to sort out.

Once a fat guy called Pickles said, 'Blow this, Rice. I'm not shovelling that stuff in the rain all day. I'm going sick.'

'You can't,' I said. 'Somebody's already done it.'

Before I knew it he was lying on his back in a dirty puddle groaning: 'Boss, boss, it's me back. I can't move.'

The screw didn't look convinced but Pickles kept it up, almost laughing at times. A stretcher was called for and we had to carry him. He was kept in the sick bay for four days, being fed and looked after. The next week he arrived back on the shovelling and we all laughed to see him.

Within a few minutes he was down again. 'Boss, boss, me back, me back.'

I couldn't believe it. Surely he couldn't pull it off twice?

The screw came across. 'What's up with you, lad?'

'Me back, boss,' he groaned. It was the worst piece of acting I'd ever seen. This time he failed to keep his amusement in check and, chuckling, he emerged from his elaborate groans.

'Get up, you lazy fat slob. Stop messing me about!' roared the screw, who dragged him around, trying to get him on to his feet.

Soon Pickles was miserably working alongside us again, having been placed on report.

Meanwhile I became more depressed, hating everyone and everything. When my probation officer visited, I faced my chair to the window and ignored him until it was time for him to leave.

One day a lad ran up from behind and butted me in the ear, knocking me across a table. I turned in total shock but noticed the screws were standing back.

The lad shouted, 'Come on! Come on!'

I knew it was a setup; they wanted me to retaliate in order for me to lose more remission and have me sent to a prison.

'What are you standing there for?' I shouted at them. 'Do your job and grab him.'

They wrestled him down and dragged him away. Later I was

called to the wing governor's office, where the lad stood.

'Now, what are we going to do about this, Rice?' he asked.

'Well, I don't want him put in the block. It's a total waste of time. What does anybody learn down there? I'd rather we just let it go. I'm sick of this place and just want to get out.'

After some heated discussion it was decided that the lad should get away with it. 'But let me warn you: Put a finger near me again and I'll break both your arms. Understand?'

This incident was the turning-point for me. I now kept to myself, living in my own private misery and pain. A lot of the remission I'd previously lost was given back to me.

Years later I discovered that they'd given up trying to change me and let me go.

Release day was on the horizon. Arrangements were made for me to live back at my mother's house. She'd collect me at the gate on the day.

My desire to run mad on the streets had completely diminished. I didn't know what to do with my life. I certainly didn't want to be locked up again.

While in Borstal I discovered a talent for drawing and actually began making good money from my sketches.

I always swore that if any screw spoke to me outside the gate after release I'd give him a mouthful of abuse. When the day finally came, though, I was like a mouse walking in stunned amazement to the car. A screw on his way in to work said: 'Good luck, Ricey.'

'Yes,' I mumbled in reply. 'See ya.'

Mother had brought lovely ham rolls and some tins of lager, but I couldn't eat or drink. I just rode along in a dream.

At home, the family greeted me warmly and were supportive in every way they could. My new probation officer, Pat Halpen, was a great help, too. He found customers for my sketches and got me into his soccer team.

After years of rebellion and being hammered by its consequences, I now felt much older than my 19 years. Things were looking good for me, but would I be able to stay out of trouble?

3
Struggle for freedom

My criminal diversion had been painful for everyone, and particularly damaging for me.

My younger sister, no longer a child, was fulfilling her potential at college, studying to become a secretary. Old school friends drove by in cars they'd bought as a result of having responsible jobs, leaving me feeling even more entrenched.

I could see no path down which my future lay, let alone a clear objective. Even just going out for a drink, I realised what a great knock my confidence had taken. The bars were filled with strong young men strutting a self-assurance that was once mine. Compared to them I was a shivering wreck, nervous about all sorts of imaginary things.

Each fortnight when my unemployment cheque arrived, the money was spent on a night out to a couple of pubs and a club. The drink gave me the confidence to mingle, talk to girls and throw off my anxieties. My mother said I should make better use of the money, buy a watch or some clothes. She was right, but these escapades were the only freedom from my misery as a has-been failure.

The need to be a somebody or part of something was strong. The selfish, uncaring attitude I'd displayed for so long came back to haunt me.

'I'm a fit young man with good looks. Surely somebody must want me,' I thought. During these depressions my heart cried out for a woman. Even a much older woman would do, just as long as she *wanted* me.

'Where's happiness? Where's satisfaction?' I'd ask myself.

Employment was hard to come by so I began spending my afternoons either sketching or out walking.

As I arrived home one afternoon my mother said, 'An old friend of yours called here today. Do you remember Denny?'

'Yeah, course I do,' I answered.

'Well, he said he'd call back tonight.'

I was thrilled that somebody was looking me up. None of the old crowd knew where I was living. Denny must have worked hard to track me down.

When he arrived I was surprised how tall he'd grown and how deep his voice had become. My memory was of the young-looking kid I'd dumped at the precinct five years before.

We went out for a drink and talked about the things we'd been up to since we last met. Denny had moved south to Sunninghill, Berkshire, where he had a job and a place to live.

'Why don't you come back with me? I'll get you a job easily enough,' he said.

I was excited at the prospect and took up his offer. My family, who were concerned about me, were equally as happy to see me get a break.

Within two weeks I arrived by bus at my destination, but Denny, who was due to meet me, was nowhere to be seen. I phoned a number he'd given me and his sister-in-law came to pick me up. Denny arrived later, looking bedraggled. He'd overslept following a lunchtime drinking session.

The following day I met the family in whose house we were to lodge. They were great people, living in a big house in a well-heeled neighbourhood. Within a few days I secured a job as a packer in the dairy produce plant where Denny worked in Bracknell.

Keeping busy every day and living in such pleasant surroundings felt so good. The landlady introduced me to cryptic crosswords, which I was surprisingly good at. We spent many pleasant afternoons trying to complete them.

I worked lots of overtime, which helped me afford new clothes and plenty of nights out. My whole outlook took an upturn during that summer. Future plans included buying a car and taking foreign holidays.

Denny and I had many good times, making people laugh at work or in the local pub. If anything, we took things a little too far, constantly pushing the limits of outrageous behaviour. A favourite gag was to back the motorbike into an open shop doorway and rev exhaust fumes everywhere before taking off. Occasionally, we'd have to run away following a prank, and were almost caught because of our laughing.

Having to depend on Denny for a lift into work each day was a drawback. It was a 14-mile round trip with no bus service. Waking him up was a nightmare, which often ended in an argument. He was the only person I was close to, and he could cope with argument.

We were popular with our workmates and constantly had girls to take out. But the bosses were wary of our slapstick lifestyles. We clocked on at 6 am one day, having come straight from a nightclub. Both of us were drunk and found it hard to stay awake.

I got on with a busy job in order to stay alert, but after an hour or two Denny was found sleeping in a bed he'd made out of boxes. He was sacked off the shift and placed on permanent nights.

Without my pushing him, he began taking nights off. My job drifted in the same direction owing to punctures on my bike and bad weather. I got so drunk one night that the police arrested me for sleeping on the pavement. My intention was to keep it from my landlady but, after a fine in court the following morning, I came out to find her waiting to give me a lift home. She wasn't bothered at all, but I felt uncomfortable as I'd also fallen behind with the rent.

Denny and I sat up late one night sharing a bottle of whisky while lamenting the backward slide our behaviour had taken after such a good start. We had such fun together but also seemed to be bad for each other. Occasionally we'd returned to the lodgings drunk and, while nobody said anything, we knew it was wrong.

We opened another bottle and played some Stranglers records while talking. One song we liked was called *Don't Bring Harry*. To us, Harry was the ugly side of a personality that can emerge through drink—a spoiler. Before going out, one of us would often sing the short chorus as a warning to the other:

Don't bring Harry.
I don't need him around.

As often happens when the drink's gone, a craving develops for more. This was one of those occasions. We were in high spirits. 'Come on,' I said. 'I know where we can get some more.'

We rode on the motorbike to a nearby liquor store intent on breaking the front window. Scrabbling around in the dark for a good rock proved difficult until I had a brainwave.

'I know,' I said. 'Take me back to the house. I've got just the thing.'

We rode back precariously. Then I jumped off, ran inside and re-emerged with a large can of sliced pears.

'This'll do it,' I declared.

'What is it?' asked Denny.

'Never mind. Drive on.'

When we arrived I stepped off the bike and launched the can straight through the window, making a terrible racket. Heads appeared at the upstairs window, but I calmly chose my poison and sped away.

A car driven by a man who'd witnessed the incident gave chase. In shaking him off we drove off-track from the house on to a main road. Before travelling far, we were pulled up and arrested by the police. This time we really *had* gone too far.

After being charged and given bail I left the area, heading this time into London. It was amazing how quickly I felt lonely, so I decided to try my luck down in Torquay.

At first I made plenty of superficial contacts in pubs, but once the money ran out so did the friends. I felt myself inextricably drawn back to the streets of my early youth. 'At least I'll have some companionship,' I thought.

Emotions of failure rose as I slipped into the downward trend. I'd once read in a book that when a man is running in despair, he'll eventually seek out a place from his past where he last felt warm and safe.

Arriving back on Merseyside, feeling a failure, I instinctively picked up where I'd left off years before, except this time I was more cynical, violent and moody.

Turning to strong drink and drugs accelerated the downhill

process, dragging me further into the pit of disaster. I shacked up with a girl I'd known for years. But just trying to go steady with her seemed to expose all my insecurities.

She became pregnant so we decided to marry. The arrangements were quickly made and we were all set for a cheap registry office job. Deciding to marry was like grasping at straws. I hated the area where we lived, hated the lifestyle we were into and could see no hope for a good future. Money for drink and drugs was all I wanted, escaping reality was my daily occupation.

The night before we were due to marry I was arrested for beating up a man outside a nightclub. It was a serious incident which put paid to any hope of reaching the registry office. The magistrates amazingly granted me bail, after which I went on a rampage of crime and violence.

The police, wanting to question me about various incidents and jumping bail, caught me a few weeks later in a roadblock late at night. As before, I admitted everything, wanting to be washed clean of all the consequences of my crimes. The depression of the later stages of Borstal enveloped me immediately as I arrived again at Risley.

After being moved from one prison to another to face more charges, I was eventually sentenced to two and a half years.

Prison life was gloomy and boring. Prison was filled with people who hated the system but were incapable of escaping it.

Suicide became a stronger alternative than ever; hope for my future looked grim. My whole mind and emotions became consumed with hate. The family cheerfully kept up contact, though through utter shame I hardly felt able to write. My ex-girlfriend, who was now ready to give birth, had kept up regular contact. Her loving letters eventually broke through my hard indifference, bringing from me a commitment to get back together.

When I was being considered for parole, I was looked on favourably. My behaviour had been very quiet—subdued mostly. The family supported me and I had an apartment to move into with a girlfriend and child. When eventually I was granted parole, instead of being joyful with the news of an early release, my mind filled with fear and doubt. The memories of past failures and the accompanying pain came back in a flood.

During a visit from my mother, girlfriend and baby, they congratulated me warmly on receiving parole. But through the talk my mother could discern my uneasiness. I was unhappy and she knew it.

A week later she came back alone.

'I don't want to live in that apartment. We only get on when we're apart, and I can't give that baby a life,' I said.

'Well, we can work something out once you're free, son,' she said hopefully.

'Look, it'd be better if I knocked back the parole and came out on my own terms at the end of the sentence. I can make it.'

'But shouldn't you just get yourself free and then sort it out, son?'

The worry of seeing me spend any more time inside was etched across her face. She'd already commented with concern that I'd lost so much weight and appeared grey-faced.

Over the following weeks I was unable to make up my mind. Although I thought of refusing parole, it'd be a painful decision and cause more anxiety to those who loved me. So I just let things ride along as they were until parole release day.

It was a cold, dark winter's morning when I stepped out on to the wet busy street. The prison door slammed behind me as I got in step with the people headed down the main street to the train station.

The journey was an unhappy one, kept alive only by the letters I'd had from Denny recently. He'd voluntarily gone to prison to pay off some fines but was all set for a new life over in Paris after release. I was interested in going with him but would need to finish my parole period first.

My mother and sister collected me from the station and took me to the apartment. It was in the middle of a rough housing estate where many of my fights and troubles had taken place. I felt trapped and afraid.

It was impossible to see where my future lay. One day at a time was bad enough. I had some money stashed away and began spending it on drink. Each day I got drunk, sometimes crying over a bottle of gin.

'You should sod off to Paris with Denny when he gets out,' said my girlfriend. 'You're a nuisance around here. I had everything worked out until you came back.'

My conditions on parole were quite restrictive in terms of moving address, so I had to stay put until it expired. The things I'd longed so much for while inside were now hardly satisfying.

One night, while drunk, I roamed the streets until the early hours, letting my mind wander all over the place. Staggering home, I bumped into a guy who invited me in for a drink. It was obvious he was a homosexual, but with the alcohol I was able to overcome any fears and sat there talking. He offered to let me sleep on the couch. I accepted and he disappeared upstairs to bed. I thought about robbing him but fell asleep.

In the morning he brought me a cup of tea, then leaned towards me with obvious intentions. It sickened me, so in a flash I decided to rob him and grabbed his throat tightly. He screamed and thrashed about more than I'd expected.

While we fought, his dog, which was locked in the kitchen, began leaping at the door wildly. The man was desperately trying to get to it for protection as I rained punches on him.

Pinning him down, I said, 'Look, stop fighting. I'll go and leave you alone, you stupid idiot.'

But he kept struggling. I couldn't just run, because he'd let the dog out into the street to get me.

'I'll have to knock him out,' I thought. After hitting him with the underside of a glass bottle, it broke and he slumped. There was blood all over me. The dog was still going wild and I had to get out quickly. I emptied his pockets, cleaned myself up a bit, then left.

I arrived by taxi in Chester, bought a new shirt and got washed up. Moving from pub to pub I killed time until evening before ringing to see what was happening. My sister answered.

'Jimmy!' she cried. 'The police have been here looking for you. What've you done? They're saying terrible things about you.'

'Looking for me?' I exclaimed. 'It must be a mistake. I'll go and see them.' My instinct was to calm her fears, though the news she brought meant the end for me.

'Listen, I must go. The money's run out. Don't worry. Everything's all right.'

I rang off. Sickness filled my whole being. My life was destroyed. All hope was gone—my plan now was to kill myself.

I didn't fancy anything painful so I got hold of some powerful pills and a bottle of whisky. With the remaining money I'd visit a good restaurant for a slap-up meal, then kill myself in the park.

The food was good and I had fun with two girls who joined me at the table.

Afterwards, I made my way to a quiet corner of a big park and sat taking handfuls of pills and swigs of whisky. When it was all gone I lay on a bench feeling dizzy. I really *did* want to die, but soon I felt sick and vomited everything up.

I began picking half-dissolved tablets out of the mess and eating them again in desperation. But it soon became clear that I wasn't about to die. If anything, I felt as well as could be.

'What an idiot! I can't even kill myself,' I cursed.

Later, during the early hours of the morning, the police arrested me in a car with a woman I'd contacted. I'd been out of prison for only 10 days.

In the police cell I sank deeper and deeper inside myself, feeling totally unable to cope with the situation.

The police treated me as though I were a violent psychopath, keeping me under tighter security than I'd ever known. They told me that the man I'd attacked was still in a serious condition and might yet die.

When my mother visited the cells in the morning I could see in her eyes that she was looking at a lost son. There was nothing left for me to say to her. My life had said it all; it was a deeply tragic moment between us.

On the way to Risley the police taunted me, rooting for an excuse to beat me up. They handcuffed me to the van bars and threatened to kill me, knowing that, with my record for violence, they could blame me for starting it.

When we arrived, I was kept in a sweat-box, a tiny cell usually reserved for sex offenders for their own protection. Once out of there, I had to strip off in front of all the reception screws before dressing in prison garb. Instead of putting me into the 'cage' ready for a move on to the landings, I was taken to another door. Three screws stood outside with a dog, ready to lead me across a big yard towards the hospital.

'Why are you taking me over there?' I asked.

'Just shut up and keep moving,' one of them said, wheeling the dog round and making it bark furiously just inches from my face. 'Any lip from you, Rice, and you've had it, so move.'

As we walked across that dark, wet square in the drizzle I realised how wildly out of proportion my reputation had grown. To the authorities I was a heartless, unpredictable thug. Yet inside I simply felt lost, afraid and desperately lonely.

Once we'd reached the hospital wing they took me to a strange-looking cell block.

'Clothes off!' barked the screw.

'What?' I asked incredulous.

They backed off a little, again seeming to expect me to launch an attack.

'Just do it,' said one of them, drawing a batten from his pocket. 'Any trouble from you in here and you'll get a good kicking, followed by the liquid cosh [an injection].'

They handed me a massive pair of unrippable shorts and pushed me into the cell. It was the worst cell I'd ever been in and it helped to drag me down to the lowest point of my life.

Some rough canvas was my bed. The plastic pot was overflowing with somebody else's stinking excreta. I could see snot and spit up the walls, along with smears of blood. There were no windows, and the light was kept permanently on. I was an animal in a dirty cage.

'Is this my life? Is this all it amounts to?' I asked myself in horror. It was devastating to have desired so much to be free and yet have failed so badly. I curled up on that filthy canvas, cursing the day I'd been born. This time I'd definitely kill myself.

When I was unlocked, the screws lined the corridor and kept a close watch on the bathhouse as we used the toilets and washed. It was my first look at my fellow occupants, and what an assortment they were! Many walked around unshaven and undressed, drugged up to the eyeballs. Others wore long shorts and haunted expressions. None of us were allowed any clothes or possessions in case we killed ourselves or somebody else. I learned later that everybody on this wing was in for murder or extreme violence.

After washing, I stole half a tube of toothpaste and a small piece of wood. In my cell I stripped the tube down and inserted it into the wood, making a sharp knife.

'Right, I'll keep this until I can stand no more, then I'll cut my throat.'

Suicide was no dramatic step. Life was so painful that cutting my throat was only a small thing.

One day a little lady in grey visited the cell. She was from the prison church.

'Is your name Rice, James Rice?'

'Yeah, why?'

'I just need to take some details. Now, are you Catholic, Protestant, Jewish or another faith?'

'Is that all you've come to ask?' I answered. 'I'm not any religion. I *hate* religion, so get lost.'

She looked ruffled. 'Can't you just tell me what you are?'

'No, go away. I'm nothing.'

The following day a priest came to ask if there was anything he could do for me.

'Yeah,' I said. 'Find out why they're keeping me in this nuthouse.'

He promised he would, but I never saw him again.

I survived hour by hour, day by day, week by week, until they moved me back on to an ordinary wing. Living on there was so easy by comparison.

I knew Denny was inside there somewhere, serving time for his fines, so I hoped to get a message to him. One day a work party arrived to unblock our sinks and there he was lending a hand.

'Denny!' I said, punching his arm.

He looked at me in shock.

'Why are you in here? What's happened? I thought you were out.'

'I beat a guy up quite bad. I think I'm gonna get a long time for it. I was only out for 10 days.'

He looked surprised and downhearted.

I grabbed him by the shirt and said laughingly, 'Don't go worrying about me, Denny boy. I'll be back, no matter how long it takes. Nothing can keep me down. You just get over to Paris and I'll follow you across one day.'

A screw came to move me on.

'You're unbelievable, Jim,' were Denny's parting words.

Back in my cell I knew my words were just brave talk. There was no evident way for me to get through this alive.

When my girlfriend visited, I told her to get out and never visit me again. 'Get on with your own life and forget me for your own good,' I said before walking out.

On the day before my 21st birthday I received a four-year sentence for grievous bodily harm and was taken to Walton Jail in Liverpool.

4
Breaking-point

Four years was better than expected, but it still seemed a crushing amount.

A glimmer of optimism arrived, however, by way of the two characters I shared a cell with on that first night.

One of them, aged about 30, had recently received eight years for aggravated burglary. He was thoroughly miserable, having left his wife and young children to fend for themselves. It was impossible for him to come to terms with such a big sentence after what started out as a simple burglary.

The other man was a short, stocky gangster, well known in the Liverpool underworld as an armed robber. He was serving 15 years for a bank job and seemed to be as happy as could be.

'I've only got four left,' he enthused. 'It's all over for me,' he said, rubbing his hands together.

The 32 months I'd have to serve seemed minuscule by comparison. It wasn't the time that hurt me so much as the complete and utter failure. No matter how I detested the system or how hard I tried to clean up my act, the results were always the same. Those chains that bound me to this way of life were unbreakable.

I could see the same in the lives of the men around me. They were caught in this web. An air of deadness swirled around the landings wherever they congregated. Each cell housed stories of broken families, abuse, violence, alcoholism, rejection, drug addiction, abandonment, greed, evil, failure and often innocence.

Any freshness brought in by new staff was soon choked out by the stagnant routine of indifference and mutual hatred. It was them and us, two monsters locking horns in a futile contest, a power game where any notion of rehabilitation was left on the idealistic pages of Home Office reports.

After only one night we were split up to share cells with people doing similar sentences. My new cellmate, Frankie, was doing four years for stealing wagons of meat from the docks. He was a professional who talked very little about his criminal activities.

We got on fairly well and settled down to do our bird (sentence) without attracting trouble. We worked in a tailor's shop with a hundred other men, manufacturing prisoners' clothing. My job was to iron shirt collars all day before they were sewn on. The bored men amused themselves with illegal gambling, drug smuggling, practical jokes and gossip.

After lunch we were let out to walk around the exercise yard for fresh air—two paths going clockwise were split by another going anticlockwise. The view was of screws standing guard beneath the towering dark walls of the cell blocks.

We walked in aimless circles, mumbling in hunched-up groups. If it rained we stayed inside, sometimes not getting out for days. Morning, afternoon and evening we were unlocked for 'slop out'. A whole landing would be let out to place their metal trays outside the door, empty plastic pots of urine, use the toilet quickly, then get back in the cell.

The slop-out area was small and overcrowded. It always stank horribly and was degrading enough to spark the occasional frustrated punch-up.

Work-outs in the gym offered some relief from the daily grind, but within a few weeks I was banned. My aggressive attitude crept into everything, causing the gym staff to become increasingly worried about the possibility of violence. The last straw came when I removed a steel bar from the dumbbell weights and toted it around as a weapon.

This forced me to keep fit by completing a vigorous work-out in the confined space by my bed each night. It was a combination of hundreds of press-ups and sit-ups followed by stretching and a tough ballet routine for legs.

Being fit was one of the only labels anybody could wear. All other forms of identity had been removed, even your name. Keeping fit, strong and muscular kept up pride and acted in defiance of the stagnating routine that threatened to smother the life out of us.

Frankie received an oil-like substance from a friend who smuggled drugs worldwide. It was powerful stuff and could be mixed with ordinary tobacco without detection. I followed my evening work-outs with a cold wash from two big jugs of water, then smoked a long, cool joint and got stoned.

Meanwhile, Denny had been released from Risley and had made his way to Paris. His irregular letters were a ragged assortment befitting his approach to life.

Although my replies appeared quite casual, they were drawn up with all the expert craftsmanship present only in the loneliest of people. My aim was to reach through him into the awareness of those around him, preferably a female. I presented a frivolous attitude towards my sentence, mocking its small hold on my unshakeable personality. This was spiced with the ability to make him laugh. Maybe somebody would become intrigued by the source of his mirth.

This picture I painted was a lie; the sentence was destroying me, and my unhappiness deepened as each day passed me by.

Some prisoners were prescribed powerful drugs to keep them calm. I began buying them in a further attempt to neutralize the despair. Initially, it was cosy to saunter around like a zombie for days, but after a couple of weeks I began to spiral into deep depressions. I walked around in a state of high tension, my temper flaring up for the most trivial of reasons.

Sometimes the screws wouldn't unlock me when they unlocked the other prisoners. Instead, they'd bring me out alone to ensure there was no trouble.

Frankie convinced me that I ought to stop taking drugs because of the effect they were having. It needed all my willpower to stop. I almost crawled up the walls, such were the terrible aches for more.

Being unlocked separately and banned from the gym were signs of the direction my reputation had taken. It made me realise how different I appeared on the outside compared with the reality on the inside. It reminded me, too, of how, despite my efforts to go straight and stay out of jail, I'd fallen into their grasp again and again. There seemed to be forces at work within my personality that overpowered my good intentions.

These unhappy thoughts received a lift one afternoon with the unexpected arrival of a letter from Paris, written by a lady called Genevieve. It seemed a miracle that my scheme had borne fruit. I was thrilled. The letter itself didn't contain a great deal, but that was of no concern.

Resisting the urge to reply immediately, I delayed, allowing myself time to compose a steady response, written with all the tact I could muster.

Before long our correspondence became regular. The colourful postcards she enclosed brought a flicker of light to my gloomy world.

It was around this same time that I overheard a conversation in the workshop that caught my attention. A new guy was telling his friends about the prison he'd just been transferred from. It had good food, lots of freedom and plenty of sport. And an effort was made to help the men sort out their lives.

Later, while having a smoke in the toilets, I asked him about it. 'Hey, mate, what's this prison you were talking about?'

'It's great,' he said. 'Everybody speaks on first-name terms, including the screws. It's a therapy place where you have to sit in groups and talk, but the rest of the time's easy.'

'How do you get there?'

'Just see the doctor. Tell him you're cracking up. They might send you there.'

'Why'd you get sent back here?'

'We were caught making wine. So they kicked us out,' he laughed.

I despised him for ruining such a great opportunity for himself.

'What's this place called, anyway?' I finally asked.

'Grendon,' he answered, putting out his cigarette and disappearing back on to the shop floor.

The thought of going to this Grendon place began to play on my mind constantly. Eating good food sounded fantastic, as did sport, fresh air and fair treatment. The therapy seemed a weird thing. Although I'd become sceptical about finding a solution to my life, the prospect of being helped was quite an attraction. Frankie gave me no chance of making it, saying it was too much of a long shot, but still my name went down to see the doctor.

The doctor listened impatiently as I complained that nothing was being done to help sort out my life.

'I don't want to be in these stupid places all my life,' I said.

He offered me medication, which I refused. Then he put my name forward to see a psychiatrist. Things seemed to be moving.

On the day of my appointment to see the shrink, I turned up stoned on cannabis. It took all my powers of concentration to keep from slumping into a happy daze. After reading my reports and asking a few innocuous questions, the shrink closed the interview. I returned to the daily routine without knowing how things had really gone.

A week later they told me that, despite a six-month waiting-list for Grendon, I'd be transferred there within six weeks. It was astonishing. Frankie could hardly believe I'd done it.

This was the first time I'd felt excited about anything in a long time. My transfer date soon arrived and, knowing that my new prison would offer a much better life, I left all my personal belongings to Frankie.

They transferred me in a taxi, handcuffed to a screw. It was a treat driving through the city streets towards the motorway just seeing everything. The two screws told the driver to pull up outside a pub while they removed my handcuffs for comfort. The prospect of breaking free shot through my mind, but memories of past disasters on the run put me off. Instead, I sat back and made the most of the long journey. For some unknown reason, this was the first time I'd felt relaxed while being taken to an unfamiliar institution.

On my arrival, Grendon looked much like any other prison. But once inside, the difference was obvious. Gone was the intimidating reception procedure synonymous with entry into a prison. The staff and cons (prisoners) were easy-going and friendly, and they spoke on first-name terms.

After I'd changed my clothes, a screw accompanied me to the

induction wing. This was purely because I didn't know the way; normally he'd have just let me go alone.

Another screw introduced himself by his first name and showed me to a cell.

'Unpack your things, then make your way down to the office, if you would, Jimmy,' he said, leaving me with the door unlocked.

Over the years I'd become used to communicating with screws in a particular kind of way; this friendly approach was very disarming.

I unpacked slowly, feeling a warm glow of pleasure at being here. Then I shut the door behind me, making my way to the office. The officer came out towards me.

'We don't lock doors during the day, Jim,' he said. 'Too much like hard work,' he laughed, leaving it ajar.

As we walked down the corridor, my stomach tensed up in fear at having my things stolen. In prison you never give an opportunity for anybody to steal anything.

That old fable claiming there to be honour among thieves is a load of garbage. I've seen cons stealing from each other too many times to believe in romanticism. I stood by the door while the officer asked questions and filled in forms behind his desk.

Each time he lowered his head to write, I arched back to keep an eye on my cell along the corridor. There didn't seem to be anybody around but I wasn't taking any chances. The relaxed atmosphere exposed all my hyped-up fears, making me feel completely out of place.

During that first week I was placed on an assessment programme of IQ tests, fitness exams, interviews, initiative tests and medicals. The screws made it clear that Grendon wasn't a nuthouse—the main criterion for acceptance was normality.

I wanted to stay, but behind the scenes there was considerable difference of opinion about whether to keep me or reject me.

'He's too aggressive, too entrenched in his ways, impossible to change,' said some.

'He doesn't listen to anybody. His influence on the other men would be far too negative,' said others.

However, two senior doctors saved the day.

One reported, 'He's intelligent, and this intelligence will help him to see that he must change, and then he will.'

The other, an oddball Australian psychologist who was second in command, said, 'This guy tells us he listens to John Peel on the radio. That means a lot in my book, so I say he stays.'

This meeting took place in private, of course. The details of it were revealed to me a long time after. I never did understand the John Peel factor!

They decided to place me back on a young men's wing, which enjoyed more intensive therapy than any other.

There were five groups, each consisting of six lads, who met for an hour every weekday morning along with an officer and sometimes a psychologist. In the afternoon the whole wing gathered to feed back what had happened in the groups.

It was quite daunting having to talk openly about sensitive issues with the prospect of people chipping in with comments.

My initial attitude was to enjoy all that Grendon had to offer, sidestep the therapy and breeze through my sentence. Escaping the savage drudgery of the big prison system had been an incredible achievement. I was going to make the most of it.

Unlike the case with other prisons, sex offenders, child molesters and other types of prisoner usually kept segregated for their own protection were all lumped together here. The rules against violence and intimidation were strictly enforced by the prisoners themselves.

The system forced people to be accountable for their behaviour, preventing bullies from believing they had the right to dominate anyone they chose.

It was interesting to see a big shot being challenged by a small person about his abusive attitude or something similar. The big guy often began his defence by blaming everybody else, but soon the group or wing-meeting would put the onus back on him. He was abusive; it was *his* problem.

People like me who weren't used to being accountable to anybody found it difficult to keep calm under the pressure and often burst out in aggression. This usually got me into a worse mess than I'd been in the first place, and it wasn't long before I began to relate to many of the things the other lads shared. I had a growing respect for their honesty and wondered whether my own secret identity would stay intact or the truth about me become known.

I began to wonder which parts of my personality could be shared with the group. I faced them one morning, raising my hand to use some time.

'Sure, Jimmy, fire away,' they said.

Suddenly I felt afraid. Was I making a mistake here? With arms folded tightly and eyes fixed on the floor, I said, 'Sometimes when a fight's going to start I get scared.'

There! It was out. This morsel had taken me all my courage to say. In the seconds it took before anyone spoke I felt small and stupid.

'Do you mean other people's fights or those you're involved in?' asked the screw.

'Fights I'm involved in,' I said. 'Sometimes when a person fronts me up for a fight I get really nervous.'

We discussed it for a while. The other lads were helpful by admitting to having the same emotions. Afterwards, it seemed like I'd hardly talked about anything of great substance, but to me it had been a giant leap, my first dip in the pool after circling it for weeks.

Being honest in this way left me feeling good, even clean in a way. So it wasn't long before I identified another item worth discussing. A feeling of moving in the right direction began to grow within me, bringing a fresh glimmer of hope to my previously dim horizon.

Genevieve continued to write, telling me more about herself, while I traced my steps along the therapeutic journey in reply. I wanted to share some hope with my family but felt that all words of promise had been exhausted through a succession of past failures. Action would speak louder than words.

Keeping fit, eating good food and the feeling of achievement did wonders for me. I couldn't imagine having to go back into the

Victorian prison system again. My sights were now upwards.

My willingness to be open brought its share of problems. After talking through sensitive issues, I was often left feeling vulnerable, especially by those unwilling to contribute, who sat back looking smug. Pressing on meant breaking an invisible but strong accord with those who maintained their manufactured tough-guy images while I rattled the bars of my own.

Some began to despise me, viewing my progress as a threat to their defences. But I couldn't stop. Therapy provided the only area of achievement in my life, achievement I had sorely missed and desperately needed. The loss of popularity in gaining it was a heavy and unexpected price to pay. Being seen as a traitor to the cause made the journey a lonely one.

Following lunch each afternoon we spilled out into a big yard to play soccer, during which the lads worked off a lot of steam. Although I enjoyed playing, on many occasions I chose to walk around alone, thinking to myself.

In the distance I could see a hill. I often viewed my progress as having to scale a similar height. On my slope, however, progress was achieved at a high cost. In order to gain one foot of ground I'd have to sink down 19, then come up 20. The going down represented submerging into the labyrinth of my fiery heart to rummage through festering sores. Coming up meant clawing to rediscover my identity through layers of fear, doubt, vulnerability and insecurity. The process was exhausting and opposed to my natural instincts of self-preservation.

It came as some relief to hear from Genevieve that she'd be coming over to visit me soon. The thrill of anticipation kept me going through the weeks before her visit. Having never seen a photo, I'd built up a mental picture of her life and looks. I already knew she was single, 10 years older than me, had a good job, lived in the city and liked adventure.

Compared to English girls, she expressed a laid-back attitude towards relationships, something I presumed to be a European continental feature. She implied that her visit was primarily to London, with me tagged on to the end, but I knew she liked me.

On the day of her visit the sun shone beautifully, making her choice of floral dress seem just right. She looked different from what I'd expected, and, as is often the case with a person waiting in over-eager expectation, not as good as I'd hoped.

It's amazing how, after looking forward to seeing somebody so much, you then struggle for things to say. Having to squeeze communication into a rigid time-slot cramps natural conversation.

After overcoming the initial difficulties in understanding each other's dialects, we got on fine. Our friendship, which had grown steadily for a year, was firmly enhanced by those two hours together. It was great for my ego having Genevieve visit all the way from Paris. I felt like a real *somebody*.

Following her visit I got back to the group work, raring to go. Everything was thrown into the therapy, including one revelation that was the toughest of all. Ever since my time in detention centre I'd been plagued with occasional homosexual thoughts. The nearest I'd ever come to telling anybody was while drunk with Denny one night years before. Since then I'd carried it around like dirty baggage, feeling increasingly confused and even guilty.

It was another example of how little other people knew about the real me. Everything was locked up on the inside. Just the thought of telling the group terrified me. But such was my determination to find answers that I came to them one morning ready to spill the beans. The interpretation I placed on it was that I was bisexual, and that's what the group were told.

There was a stunned silence, during which I thought I'd made a terrible mistake. The first person to speak was a guy who usually didn't say much, but who normally just got angry and swore abuse.

'I really admire you for saying that, Jim,' he said.

The other lads spoke up, too, bringing a good round of conversation. Before long, four of them confessed to having felt exactly the same from time to time. It was a refreshing meeting during which we were able to laugh and get some perspective on the matter.

Revealing it to the whole wing on feedback during the afternoon was equally as tough. As time passed, I came to realise that I wasn't bisexual at all, but had simply experienced a thought pattern fairly common in most young people.

My strong efforts to find a solution to my life drew the attention of two screws who were religious. I enjoyed chatting with them because they were approachable. But I couldn't understand how they could be so easily hoodwinked into church stuff. Having to sing dreary hymns to a boring organ in a cold, echoey church seemed ridiculous, besides having a priest say things nobody understood.

One of them pushed his luck one day by giving me a book to read written by an ex-New York gang leader called Nicky Cruz, who'd ended up believing in God. 'You'll relate to this man very much, Jimmy,' he said, looking triumphant.

I was irritated by his clumsy attempt to lure me in this direction. 'Does he think I'm so stupid?' I thought.

I read the book with a determination to hate it. The first half of it about the gangs was good, and the story of his conversion to Christianity was interesting, too, but I was never going to admit it.

Strolling into the office one evening I slapped it down on the desk and said, 'The book ends up crap. If this guy's supposed to be so tough, why does he need God? I don't need no God. You get this Nicky Cruz over here and we'll see how tough he is.'

I spun on my heels and left without waiting for a reply. In truth, I admired Nicky Cruz for his honesty, but none of that religious stuff was for me.

Despite the great effort I'd put in since arrival a year ago, nagging old feelings of hatred and violence began to re-emerge. Therapy had made no impression on the aggression, fear and insecurity that bound me. It seemed that 'Harry' was still around.

The staff were getting into the habit of holding me up as an example to the other lads. 'Look at Jimmy Rice,' they'd say. 'He's worked hard, he'll make a success of his life—and you could do the same.'

These general assumptions about my future were annoying, although it was easy to see why they were made. I was polite, patient, stood up for standards and was willing to listen to other people's problems.

Frustration began boiling into anger at my inability to overcome the destructive side of my personality. Anxiety about the future returned with the realisation that massive hurdles had to be overcome.

I decided to bring these concerns to the wing meeting and set the record straight. The staff and lads sat on chairs around the dining hall sipping tea from plastic jugs, wondering what today's meeting might bring. Some looked nervous, knowing that if they were pulled up for bad behaviour the wrath of the whole wing could descend on them. My request to use 15 minutes was granted, and after a short wait I began.

'It's about the way I'm looked on by everybody. I'm sick of people using me as an example saying I've got it all worked out, because I haven't. I may walk around being polite and friendly, but the truth is I hate the guts of nearly all of you. If I had half the chance I'd have punched most of you straight through the wall by now.'

I glanced around at the surprised faces. 'I don't just get annoyed when you do irritating things. I want to knock the *hell* out of you.'

I could sense disappointment around the room.

'What am I going to do out on the streets after my release when prison rules and regulations are gone? I've acted as nice as pie in here to avoid being thrown out into a big prison again, but that's not how I'm feeling deep down.'

I paused, but still no response came.

'Listen,' I went on, 'the thing is, I don't want to hate anyone or hit anyone. It just wells up inside. I can't help it. I want to like people, to be genuine and enjoy life, but I have to wrestle every day with what's inside me.'

I turned to a psychologist across the room and asked: 'I've tried everything in here. I've torn myself apart, but this hate remains. Where does it come from? Why does it just barge in on my life? *Tell me how to get rid of it.*'

All eyes turned to him as he shifted uncomfortably while considering his answer. He talked about 'switching on to happy thoughts' and 'thinking positive' as if we could shift moods like switching TV channels.

As he spoke, people turned away one after another, disappointed in what they heard. The thing that struck me about his answer was that I knew *he* didn't believe it himself!

As he trailed off, I spoke again. 'The best way for me to describe my situation is to say that I'm stuck inside a robot. I've programmed myself to respond to situations in such a calculated way that nobody could ever know what I'm really like. When anything happens, the robot answers too quickly, leaving my true feelings bunged up on the inside.'

Nobody knew what to say and I didn't really expect a response. It just felt good to clear the air and be honest.

That wing meeting proved to be a turning-point for me in Grendon. It was clear that psychology alone couldn't answer the deep problems troubling my life.

That night in my cell, my faith in therapy seeped away like sand from an egg-timer.

5
Rescued

I began examining various eastern religions in the hope of finding the peace I sought.

After studying Zen Buddhism and practising meditation for a while, I realised it was a totally self-centred religion that didn't deal with inner badness at all. Other beliefs were attractive, but it was difficult to see the point at which the inner badness could be tackled.

One person who sat listening during the wing meetings to my frustrated comments about hate and the robot I was stuck inside was Jenny.

She was in charge of psychodrama, the switchblade of therapy. Eight of us were allocated to her class on Tuesday evenings. She was a foxy lady—small, sexy and dynamic. Most of us fancied her but were afraid to say so.

Role play was the technique she used to prise out buried problems. For example, a lad may be asked to describe in detail how conversations, arguments or general communication took place at home between himself and his mother. Jenny would ask how his mother sat, talked and walked, whether she pointed her finger, raised her voice or folded her arms. Somebody would then be selected to play 'mother' and furniture arranged to resemble that of home many years before.

It always appeared like an ill-prepared drama to begin with; the person re-enacting a childhood encounter couldn't seriously see how anything significant could take place. But when 'mother' talks, asks, behaves, stares, ignores, shouts and fires questions, the lad is inextricably drawn into a time, place and situation long since passed.

Jenny watches like a hawk, weighing every breath, noting every word, measuring every step taken down into the past. Suddenly, the lad's struggling in confusion and Jenny pounces, a bird of prey spotting the catch.

'What do you want to say?' she asks.

'I don't know,' he answers, looking worried.

'What did you do at the time?'

'I hid upstairs and cried.'

'What would you like to have said?' she urges.

'I hate her. I wanted to tell her what I think,' he says, finding courage.

'All right, let's go back through it again and give you the opportunity to say what you wanted to say.'

We begin once more, again finding it difficult to believe anything significant could happen. Jenny primes 'mother' with a few extras to throw in to help the process. The conversation's soon rattling along. It bites deep.

The lad's pulled in to a depth where his emotions can't stand much more. He pauses, lip quivering, balanced between pulling out and an emotional collapse. Jenny's on the edge of her seat.

'You don't love me. I know you don't,' he bursts out. 'You love Karen more than me. She gets sweets and presents while I'm at school, and when I come home you just tell me off.'

Tears turn into great sobs. His head drops.

'She just doesn't love me. She just doesn't love me,' he goes on in floods of tears.

Jenny flutters in, this time a dove of peace, cradling his crying head, running fingers through his hair. 'Keep talking,' she says softly. 'Tell us what's happening inside.'

We've witnessed a child, a boy all broken up. Over cigarettes and coffee the lad talks about what he's seen or realised, while Jenny tries to package the thing back together. Time's short; the lad will be alone in his cell within half an hour trying to come to terms with this experience. Jenny's philosophy appears to be one of undoing knots in the past to bring freedom in the present.

Jenny spoke to me as we got settled into our seats for our usual Tuesday session.

'Jimmy, why don't you use the group tonight to tell us more about the robot you described at the wing meeting?'

It seemed harmless enough so I agreed. After describing in more detail what I'd meant, Jenny asked: 'Would it be fair to describe your robot as a wall, Jim?'

'Yes, I suppose it would.'

'OK, why don't you go and sit in the corner while we build a wall around you with these chairs? Then you can tell us more about the wall.'

When they'd finished, she asked me to tell the group why the wall was there.

I sat thinking about this for a while without knowing exactly what to say.

'To be honest,' I said, 'this wall's here to protect me. It's protected me from being hurt physically and mentally, too.'

Jenny then asked me to tell them why I began building the wall—and when. This was more difficult to answer. I couldn't remember a time when my behaviour had been consistently genuine. Then I remembered something that happened on the school bus when I was seven or eight.

'I was just an ordinary kid like anyone else, messing about with my friends during the ride home, when suddenly I was punched to the ground. My nose was bleeding and I struggled back to me feet in sheer panic, trying to stave off the attack.

'He was a big lad but, to my surprise, I soon got the better of him. Much to my relief, the bus conductor came and dragged us apart. He told us off, stopped the bus and then threw me off.

'Although I was afraid of violence, and I didn't mean to get involved, the incident transported me from being a little nobody into something of a celebrity. I'd been involved in a *real* fight and had blood all over my face. I'd also beaten a tough-nut and been slung off the bus.'

This incident certainly wasn't the root of all my evil, but the advantages I'd taken were typical of those grasped over subsequent years. Taking the benefits of a reputation had proved to be as addictive and hard to resist as any drug.

After hearing my story, Jenny arranged us like the inside of a bus and cleverly selected a lad to play the attacker who I didn't see eye-to-eye with anyway. We ran through the incident again and again. Each time he attacked and I stayed on the floor, trying my best to act in a way that was more true to my feelings.

He taunted me more and more. I could see that, although he was only play-acting, there was a gleam of satisfaction in his eye at seeing me humbled in this way.

When Jenny thought we'd done enough, she told me to return behind my wall of chairs. As I began to rise, she said, 'No, stay down. You're no tough guy, remember. You must crawl behind your wall.'

It was the most humiliating trip across the room I'd ever made —and probably the longest.

'I don't care,' I thought. 'I'll do *anything* to break this reputation, this false image, even if it means humiliation. I want to be real; I want to be *me.*'

Sitting behind the wall felt cosy. Something stirred inside that had been missing for such a long time: I seemed a simple person, an ordinary young man, almost boring.

Jenny sent another lad to jeer at me. 'You've come to this prison with your big, tough-guy image, acting like a real somebody. Yet look at you! You're a fake, you're nothing.'

His words stung but again I ducked them, hanging on to what was real, accepting the criticism. Another was sent forward acting as a father.

'Come out, you dirty coward,' he said. 'No son of mine hides away like this. Come out and fight again. Come on.'

He began pulling the chairs away as he ranted, but still I hung on tight, refusing to move. As the last chairs were dragged away, something snapped inside. 'Harry' was back. In one movement I was up, holding the lad off the floor by his throat.

Everybody froze as I said in carefully threatening words: 'Don't you *ever* make me fight or I'll kill you stone dead.'

My words hadn't been aimed at anyone in particular, more at a thing inside.

Before being locked up for the night, we talked about the session. It'd been a frightening experience for me during which I'd caught a glimpse of my true self.

That night in my cell I felt sad at never having been that person. I really needed somebody to talk to. My emotions had been ripped apart and it was hard to get my bearings. Once more, I remembered the hill to be climbed. It was now a mountain.

All prisons have at least one character; Grendon's was Ernie, the nightwatchman. He came on duty at 9 pm when all the officers had gone home and the prisoners had been locked up. He didn't have any keys to open cells, but he had to turn a night clock at the end of each landing which recorded his hourly tour of the cells.

Nightwatchmen usually ghost around unknown and unseen, but not Ernie. He had a good word for every lad before lights off. His simple countryside accent made him a warm, grandfatherly-type figure to most of the lads, many of whom shared their news with him each week. He could be heard laughing, making his way around, talking through the crack in the doors and striking matches to keep his pipe lit.

He and I got on fine, though there were occasions when, if feeling a bit low, I pretended to be asleep, letting him pass by. After my rigours of psychodrama and general feelings of uncertainty, I once again let him pass me by. I lay in the dark listening to his simple conversation with the lad next door.

Feeling stuck for something to say, the lad asked, 'Hey, Ernie, do you believe in God?'

'Oh, yes,' he said in his country drawl. 'I read me Bible every night and say me prayers, giving thanks to God for all I've got.'

'You would!' I thought. Another brainwashed churchgoer was all we needed to hear. These stupid, old-fashioned religions annoyed me. Why couldn't people see it was all a load of fairy-stories?

Their conversation soon trailed off and, after brief chats with the remaining lads, Ernie disappeared. To my surprise, his words about thanking God kept rolling across my mind. It occurred to me that I wasn't grateful for anything. Despite my making a terrible mess of my young life there were many years left to live.

Life had been a free gift to me, yet who could I thank for it? I had talent, ability and potential, but where did it all come from?

'There must be something, Someone, who made me,' I thought, wandering up and down the cell. As I stared at the door, hands stuffed inside my pockets and bare feet on the cold floor, I decided to give thanks to the thing somewhere out there in space that had made me.

'OK, Jimmy, lad. Let's give thanks to the thing.' It seemed right, but to speak audible words seemed ridiculous. I struggled to know what to do.

'Come on, say it,' I said to myself.

Suddenly a light turned on in my head. 'Hey, this is who God is. This is the God everybody talks about.'

All I wanted to do was to say thanks—no church or religion. But again it was really difficult.

'Give God his due, Jimmy,' I said.

My head shook in disbelief. What the hell was I doing? This time I really *was* going crazy.

My face flushed with embarrassment, even though nobody was there. With my eyes looking around, I stood awkwardly and muttered, 'Thanks, God.'

Once it was out, I loosened up a little and carried on.

'Yeah, thanks, God, for my life and my health and my fitness and everything you gave me.'

Although I'd smashed the gift of a healthy young life through riotous living, it was right to be grateful for being given it in the first place.

That night, feeling clean and refreshed, I slept better than I'd done for weeks. Yet within two weeks I sat again in the darkness of the night looking out through the bars with the same unstable feelings intact.

People continued to claim that I'd done very well and would be sure to make a success of my life, but I wasn't convinced. My ship was heading towards those treacherous waters of release. On those rocks my life had been battered again and again. Nightmares, fears and uncertainties filled my mind.

'Have I done enough? Will I *ever* do enough to break free from the stranglehold my badness has on me, or will I have to commit suicide as planned from the beginning?'

As floods of concern filled my mind, I saw this vision of a mountain similar to the one I often saw from the exercise yard. From top to bottom there were thousands of problems, all of them obstructing the answer. Each one was a personal characteristic of mine. The hope I held of finding an answer was being crushed beneath the weight of it all.

Fear gripped me as a voice seemed to say, 'Even if you make it to the top, Jimmy, you'll just be ordinary, normal.'

I turned away, my heart sinking in despair as another vision came up out of the floor. This time I saw a large, black porthole with me in the centre holding filthy things to my chest. Another came up, then another. The horror of the things I held made my hair stand on end. They were manifestations of deep-rooted badness.

Suddenly, it felt as if I was falling into the blackness from where they came. Deep inside my terrified being I cried out: *'God, please help me!'*

Almost before the words were off my lips I was floating, as if a parachute had opened, my fall arrested in tranquillity. The horror was gone, to be replaced by a massive sense of relief.

As I stood there, shaken from the whole experience, great tears welled up inside. I couldn't hold them back.

I fell to my knees, pictures of all my past hurts and pain flooding through my mind. I cried every tear I'd never cried. It was as if, while gritting my teeth through the living hell of life on the streets and in prisons, a dam had built inside me. Now the dam had broken and everything was coming out.

Alongside these memories came those of past wrongs, the many mean and despicable things I'd done.

Through deep tears of sorrow I cried: 'Oh, God, I'm so sorry, I'm so sorry.'

I remained in this state for over two hours. Eventually, saturated in sweat and tears, I curled up on my bed and slept peacefully.

In the morning when the doors were unlocked I woke with a sense of freshness I'd never felt before. Politeness to the other lads rolled off my tongue with genuine ease, rather than the usual empty words. Little did I realise the kind of dimension my life had entered into. The battles ahead would be every bit as painful as the ones of the past, but for the moment this effortless glide through the day suited me fine.

I wondered how long the mood would last. Usually it came to a sudden end or drifted into a pit of depression. By lunchtime, I was still breezing along when I bumped into Gerry, one of the religious officers.

'Hi, Jim,' he said in his usual friendly manner.

'Hi, Gerry,' I replied, feeling glad to see him. 'Listen, Gerry, I want to be a Christian. What do I do? Where do I go?'

He was completely taken aback and stood in shock for a moment before responding.

'What's brought this on, Jim?'

I hardly knew myself. It'd all happened so naturally and the words had tumbled out of my mouth so unexpectedly. I quickly rattled off the story of what had happened in the cell the night before. He almost choked on his pipe. Hearing myself say it helped to bring some perspective on the matter.

'Have you got any books I could have?'

'Yes, Jim. Get some lunch and I'll show you them later.'

As I took my place in the line, my mind went back 11 years to an incident in secondary school. One afternoon every student in my year assembled in the main hall for a special presentation. I was quite excited until I realised they were handing out Gideon New Testaments. What a stupid waste it seemed!

As I walked out through the gates with a handful of friends at the end of the day, I turned to them, Bible in hand, and said, 'What do they want to go giving us these things for? What good are they?'

The others murmured in agreement.

'I'm throwing mine away. What do I want it for?' I started ripping pages out and letting them flutter on to the ground. The more I ripped out, the more surprised they became.

Sensing my friends' concern, I turned the screw. 'Come on,' I said. 'Why don't you rip yours up, too? You don't believe in God any more than I do.'

More pages fell to the ground.

'Come on,' I pressed, 'if you believe in God, keep your Bibles. But if you don't, then throw them away. What's the use of keeping them if you don't believe?'

Nobody said a word; everybody was held motionless by the challenge. Worried looks crossed their faces and I half expected a big fist to punch me from the sky.

Tossing the book into the gutter was the signal for us to move on and, typical of 11-year-olds, we were soon talking about other things, the Bible incident having been completely forgotten.

Eating lunch I felt sorry about what I'd done to that little book all those years ago. In my mind I threw up a quick message to God.

'Hey, I'm sorry about what I did. But if you give me another one, I'll take care of it this time.'

After lunch, Gerry took me to a small tea room where a large collection of books filled one wall. There were all kinds of fancy things to read, but I knew exactly what I was looking for. My eyes skimmed the shelves quickly. 'Come on, God,' I thought.

Then, suddenly, hidden among bigger volumes, I spotted a little Gideon New Testament and snatched it up in glee.

'Can I have this one?' I asked, holding it up.

'Yes,' replied Gerry, showing me another book. 'You can have this one, too, and . . . .'

'No, no,' I cut him off. 'I only want this. Can I keep it? Can it be mine?'

'Yes.' He didn't know why I wanted this book in particular but simply granted my wish.

That evening I could hardly wait for lockup time in order to begin reading, and once I got started it was hard to stop. Occasionally, I put the book down and considered what had taken place over the past 24 hours of my life. It was amazing. I'd called out to God, felt his rescue, cried my heart out, told somebody I wanted to be a Christian and was now reading the Bible, of all things!

During the following weeks I spent less and less time watching

TV or playing pool in the evenings, preferring instead to sit alone in my cell reading my Bible. Some people stopped by to ask me why, but to answer in a way they could understand was very difficult. I just said it was a great book.

I began to realise that the hope I'd been searching for had arrived. Fears about the future were being swept away by a fresh tide of optimism. Prison was over for me. I knew it with a certainty that's beyond description. My life had been rescued, a fresh start had begun. Now I'd find my place in life and succeed for certain—I just knew it.

I'd paced up and down many prison-cell floors sensing the deep frustration of never having fulfilled my potential, wasting all my talent and ability, and feeling alienated from mainstream life. But now things were going to be different. My purpose in life would be realised, my role fulfilled. It was exciting to be allowed back into the ball game.

As my new hope grew, other more vain ideas regarding the future fell away, the first of which was Paris. Going there seemed pointless. Why should I seek my hope over there when it was now in the palm of my hand? My eyes had been opened to the folly of many paths I'd previously been willing to consider.

Such was the massive change inside me that I decided to tell everybody at the wing meeting. As usual, I booked some time and sat waiting while other subjects were debated.

When it came to my turn, our elected chairman gave me the nod. 'Over to you, Jimmy.'

'Well, it's like this,' I said awkwardly. 'I'm a Christian now, a proper one.'

A silence followed during which facial expressions seemed to say, 'Yeah? So what? Why use wing time to tell us that?'

'I just thought I'd better tell you,' I said, trying to fill the gap.

More disinterested silence followed.

'OK, Jimmy, great, good for you,' said a solitary voice.

'That's it, then,' I said, feeling embarrassed and wanting proceedings to move on quickly. I suppose telling them I was a Christian was like telling them nothing at all. Many lads in jail take on new religions as a form of identity just to be *different*. What I really wanted to explain to them was the exciting change that had taken place in my life.

Having applied for parole again, I was fortunate to have my old friend, Pat Halpen, as my parole officer, and I wrote to him. We hadn't been in touch for a while so I sent him an honest account of what was going on.

We'd first met when Pat was given the dubious pleasure of being my probation officer while I was in Borstal at the age of 17. I'd hated probation people and lost no time in telling him where to go on our first meeting. However, I soon learned that he could give as good as he got; he'd call my bluff on any issue and was a genuinely helpful person.

After seeing me get locked up again following Borstal and then failing after only 10 days of parole, he could be excused for doubting my ability to make it in life. Pat knew my potential, but he feared that the corruption had consumed it like it had with so many who'd passed before me.

My letter contained more than the collection of empty promises prisoners so desperately want to believe about themselves. He shared with me quite unashamedly at a later date that the letter had reduced him to tears.

And with Pat I'm not talking about an arty social worker with CND stickers on a trendy French car. He's an ex-bus driver, an Irish-blooded Evertonian, a 6' 2" centre half who never shied out of a tackle in his life. Something of the magnitude of my change had jumped off the pages at him. *Jimmy Rice was free!*

When Denny heard that for me the old ways were finished, he wrote back with unusual swiftness, asking for a visiting order so that he could come over from France to see me. This reaction was totally out of character; for him this world held nothing of sufficient importance to raise more than a smirk.

I despatched the visiting order and looked forward to seeing him again. On the day of the visit he turned up two hours late, with only 30 minutes remaining of visiting time. I'd spent the afternoon playing pool, wondering if he was ever going to arrive. The staff allowed us some extra minutes together in view of his long journey. He looked tired, had lost weight and was bedraggled after hitch-hiking for two days.

Pat earned his crust from busking around Paris's Champs Elyses. It was a hard life, but offered excitement, freedom and, occasionally, very lucrative earnings. He hated the winters and swore each year that he couldn't face another. But many seasons were to pass before he was to seek pastures new.

It's the custom for the visitor to bring cigarettes, but this time I had to borrow one from an officer for Pat. We greeted each other warmly, then sat back looking one another over with a smile. I couldn't help but notice the difference between us: I was in great physical shape, bright-eyed and smiling, while Denny seemed drawn, tardy and unhappy.

We exchanged small talk over a cup of tea before he leaned forward in a more serious tone and asked, 'What's the score, then, Jimmy? What's been going on around here?' His smirk suggested he hoped this thing might not be real.

'I don't know, really, Den,' I said, forgetting what I'd prepared myself to say. 'I just feel different now and can't go back to my old life. It's finished.'

Looking across while blowing smoke through his teeth, he realised that my change ran deep. He'd come to Grendon doubting the possibility of my life being so radically altered, but now he could see for himself; his fears were being realised.

Our friendship was old enough to cope with the silence that followed before he carried on in his serious tone.

'Look, Jim, I've known you since we were kids and I always thought you were a nutter, a real hard case, the genuine article. As we got older, you frightened me half to death with the things you got up to. But I'm not like you. I was just pretending, hanging on to your shirt-tails trying to keep up.'

The eyes grew glassy, his voice sinking deeper with meaning.

'But now you've gone home and I'm stuck out here alone. I can't get back, Jim. . . .' He trailed off, his voice betraying the emotion of the boy I'd known so many years before.

His instinctive grasp on the gulf that separated us woke me up to its reality. He was lost—I was found; he was dead—I was alive; he was lonely—I'd come home. Denny knew that I'd always been honest about my badness, never wanting to pull the wool over anybody's eyes. If I'd been trying to kid him he'd have spotted it with those streetwise eyes in no time.

So we sat in the knowledge that our friendship would never be the same again. A part of us had died for ever. We embraced before parting and as he turned to leave I saw a sad character whose direction was lost. Although he was returning to the playground of Europe for a life that many would envy for its abandon, in the light of my freedom he was truly in chains.

Denny may never have glimpsed the darkness of his situation nor I the brightness of my own had we not sat face to face in the visiting room that day.

A few days later I received the astounding news that I'd been granted parole and would be out within weeks.

It was highly unusual for somebody who'd broken parole by committing violent crime to be given it ever again. Coupled with that, I'd failed to show up at court many times, absconded from Borstal, broken nearly all the bail ever granted and destroyed my previous parole within 10 days by committing a serious crime. As a result, I'd been told to expect nothing.

News that I'd been granted parole meant I entered a period of prison life that's without rival. Having served almost three-and-a-half years, with only a 10-day break on parole, I found those final weeks brought an increasing sense of euphoria.

Gate fever! That's what it was. I'd triumphed over the agony of arrest, charges, remand, sentencing and prison itself. Now I stood on the threshold of the greatest prize—freedom!

I attained the lofty air of veteran, looking back on tough times like an old man remembering the war. The staff became super-friendly, the world looked a nicer place. Nothing could grind me down, and I was full of charitable forgiveness to those who were less fortunate.

The memory of past release dates was bitter. Never had I hoped for so much, only to find so little. Those heady last days in the womb-like comfort of prison are a cruel preparation for the cold reality out on the street.

Many men step forth with £50 and a rail pass and are expected to build a new life. Being an ex-prisoner leaves you at the bottom of the pile, a failure not to be trusted. The world's fast; it didn't wait for me on those past occasions, and there was no celebration for my victory.

But on this occasion, thanks to God's rescue act, I felt elevated above those familiar fears. The sunshine had come out inside me. It was like starting my life all over again. I could hardly wait to get on with it.

A Christian lady called Annette urged me to make contact with a church when I got out, stressing the importance of meeting with other Christians. I'd visited the prison chapel a couple of times but they seemed to have formalised the life out of it. In the prayer group, I shared with them my excitement about Jesus, my big hero. But they, too, were pretty boring.

Through reading my little Gideon New Testament each day I came to realise that Jesus had died on the cross so that miserable people like me could be forgiven and set free. Although I couldn't prove to anybody through the Bible that Jesus could rescue lives, my experience was totally undeniable—it was real!

Before I left reception on the final day, an old lifer shook my hand and wished me well.

'Good luck, Ricey. You'll do all right out there, son. I've got a lot of admiration for you. Don't forget to have one for me.'

'No, I won't forget. Thanks. See ya!'

Leaving Grendon was almost sad. I'd been through so many dramatic experiences in there, but eventually I'd found what I'd always been looking for.

On the train home I sat opposite a delightful young lady from Bournemouth. We dropped into conversation. She was travelling up north for an interview at a university. When she asked the reason for my journey, she was fascinated to learn that I was on my way home from prison.

This led to a whole variety of questions, the answers to which amazed her more and more. As the train sped along carrying lives to an assortment of destinations, a true story of unusual content was unfolding before her very eyes. The prison gates had closed the chapter of a tempestuous life that had been rescued at the eleventh hour.

The train was pulling me along into an exciting future of boundless possibilities. What a far cry from past times, when I could be seen staring out of the window deep in thought, smoking cigarettes and sipping lager from yet another can!

The very memory of those nightmare days sent a shudder down my spine. I thanked God it was all over.

6
A daily choice

I arrived home in a more calm and settled state than on any previous occasion.

It was July; the sun shone brightly and the days were long and hot. I didn't want to rush off looking for work immediately; I needed space to gather my thoughts. In the past I'd scrambled after money through fear of an advancing tidal wave of failure, but not this time. My feet were now on solid ground—the fear was gone.

On most days over those first few weeks I packed a lunch and set off for West Kirby, a lovely coastal town on the west tip of the Wirral. At low tide I walked out across the massive expanse of sand to sunbathe behind one of the three islands off Hilbre Point.

Sitting there looking out to sea in the beautiful sunshine each day was a wonderful experience. The sun seemed to soothe my very bones. I wrote many letters out there to those left behind in Grendon, as well as to Genevieve and Denny in Paris.

Time passed by and the day soon arrived when I seriously needed to look for work. But jobs were either petty or thin on the ground. I attempted starting up a window cleaning round but failed to win enough customers. After resurrecting my drawing ability, I gained a number of commissions for sketches, but the income proved to be too slow and the work over-intense.

I'd naïvely expected my life just to slot into place without any effort. How wrong I was!

As the world woke up each morning and began operating like a big machine, everybody had a part to play. It was frustrating standing on the touchline without a role to fulfil. The need to be involved in something meaningful grew into an ache.

Annette continued to write to me. She encouraged me to join a church, stressing again the importance of meeting with other Christians. I wanted to do this, but the thought of walking into a place full of strangers was quite daunting. I kept putting it off.

Reading my little Gideon New Testament wasn't as easy as it had been in Grendon, either; there seemed so many distractions.

I tried to steer clear of alcohol but my efforts only seemed to last for about 10 days at a time. I felt disappointed and guilty because, when I was under the influence of alcohol, I swore, smoked, pursued the wrong kind of women and pushed God into the background. I nicknamed myself 'Jimmy the Ten-day Wonder'.

According to the laws of the land I was a reformed character. But somehow there seemed to be another voice speaking inside which troubled me a lot. I wondered about finding a place of my own to live and starting again. After prison I'd grown used to having my own space.

With the job market so unfruitful, I turned my attention to further education. In view of my total lack of educational and professional qualifications, it made sense to consider spending a number of years putting something together.

Pat Halpen found me a small class whose aim was to help adults brush up on maths and English, or to make a fresh start in education. After visiting the class, completing a couple of tests and finding the place friendly, I signed up to join the following week.

It was with utter joy that I got out of bed and prepared myself for class on that first Monday morning. Having somewhere to go, a task to fulfil and a part to play was a huge relief.

Riding along on the bus with school kids, workers and others who had busy days made me feel I'd joined the human race. I made a busy start and enjoyed the challenge. But my progress was interrupted after only one week by Pat, who phoned to ask whether I'd like to take part in an outdoor activity course that was starting the next day. It was hard to decide, but my teacher helped by suggesting it was an opportunity not to be missed, so I accepted.

The following day Pat took me to the Operation Drake Fellowship Centre (now Fairbridge) in Conway Street, Birkenhead. Their objective, as a result of the riots in the early 1980s, was to motivate young unemployed people from the inner cities through adventurous outdoor activities.

The staff greeted me warmly and explained that the course

would last 10 days, the first five doing local activities and the remainder camping in the Lake District.

After filling in a form, I was asked to wait in the large kitchen downstairs. Others were sitting around, too. As we hadn't been introduced to each other or given something to do, an awkward atmosphere arose. I was reminded of the many uncomfortable situations I'd experienced when entering prison reception areas.

Having waited like this for over half an hour, I decided to clear off home.

The next morning I phoned in to ask whether anything would be happening today. After their assurance that things were now in full swing, I made a return.

There were 12 of us in the group, 10 male and two female, alongside three instructors. We sped around Merseyside from one activity to another, stuffed into the back of an undersized minibus. We tried rock climbing, abseiling, shooting, canoeing, orienteering and some games.

Much of it was fun, but a running feud developed between the staff and some scallywags in the group who locked horns early on and remained that way until the end. These young tearaways made me laugh with their street cred and dirty looks. But I also feared for their futures, knowing what some of them were heading towards.

The rain came with us on the drive to the Lake District and it drizzled down on us for three days as we trekked over the hills. One lad threw his bag down and ran off during the first climb. His friends said he'd either steal a car or hitchhike back to Liverpool. But the only thing he broke into was our minibus, where we found him two days later, looking cold and miserable.

As trouble continued to flare between staff and lads, I found myself walking the middle ground, defusing situations after having gained the respect of both parties.

On our return to Birkenhead we unpacked the kit, had a cup of tea and were then presented with a smart certificate proving we'd completed the course. These were to use at job interviews to show that, despite being unemployed, we'd not been idle.

Although the course had been fraught with difficulties and

littered with flash-points, it felt a real achievement. Such was my sense of gratitude to this maverick organisation who'd reached out so freely to help that I ran a sponsored half-marathon some time later and donated the money to them.

They offered follow-up courses on sailing ships and at conservation projects in Scotland, and they made us welcome to visit the centre at any time. I declined the offer of any further activity, however, and refocused my attention on my education. Little did I realise that the first moves were being made in a plan for the next nine years of my life.

Back in class I passed with distinction two City & Guilds exams in maths, and was then encouraged to sign up for maths, English and sociology 'O' levels at Birkenhead Technical College.

As the workload grew, so did the desire to leave home for a place of my own. There were no problems—I'd simply grown used to doing my own thing over the years and needed more space.

Pat put me in touch with a housing association called Stonham which provided accommodation for people who, having made mistakes in life, were looking for a fresh start. Following an interview, they agreed to offer me a room. Unfortunately, there wasn't a vacancy in the area I preferred, so I had to wait.

'We've got a lovely place in Birkenhead, though,' they said. 'It's just been done up, overlooking the park. Why don't you try that?'

'No thanks. I'll wait.'

I wasn't familiar with Birkenhead and didn't have any family or friends there, so I dismissed the idea out of hand. Meanwhile, the struggle I was having between my new faith and my behaviour was increasing.

I woke up with a bit of a hangover one Sunday morning and felt so guilty that I ran off to the nearest church service. It was a big Anglican place where the people were quite friendly. But there was a coldness about the whole setup.

The following week I visited a less formal fellowship where things were so free and easy that people kept standing up at odd moments to shout, read the Bible or sing. Sometimes they were all doing this together, and I couldn't make head or tail of it. Three women were baptised by being completely dunked in a pool of water. It was very emotional, with people crying everywhere. Yet when I stepped back on to the pavement afterwards I felt as flat as a pancake.

I didn't know how to re-ignite the spark that had come through my experience of God in Grendon. Added to this was the frustration of waiting for the right vacancy to arise at Stonham. Each time I phoned, they continued to suggest I try the house in Birkenhead.

Eventually, out of sheer exasperation, I agreed to look at it just to shut them up. When I arrived, I found it to be a big house that had been completely refurbished. Four men would share the place, each having his own large room with a lock; the kitchen, bathroom, shower and living-room would be shared.

I took a key upstairs and went into one of the vacant rooms. As I sat on the bed, peace just flooded through me.

'I'll find my God again in this room,' I heard myself say. My mind was immediately made up to stay. Something deep inside told me that I'd found the right place. Without realising it, another piece had been placed in the jigsaw of my life.

Within a couple of weeks my mother and her husband, Frank, were helping to move me in. It was nice to see that they were as impressed with the house as I was. My room had a great view overlooking Birkenhead Park, which I used for my running. It was ideally situated, being only walking distance from college, Drake Fellowship Centre and the town centre.

The four of us who moved in struck up a good understanding, keeping the place clean and looking out for one another's needs.

The first person I got to know was Robbie. He had a wife and family but through a succession of disasters had ended up living alone. During our long conversation it came out that I'd become a Christian after serving a number of prison sentences.

Robbie said he'd had a hit-and-miss relationship with God for many years but now wanted to sort it out. He told me his brother-in-law was the part-time pastor of a small chapel in the middle of the housing estate behind our street. He suggested we try it together, so I agreed to give it a go one Sunday.

Having my own place made it easier to read my little New Testament. The excitement for life that had been dulled during the first six months of release was now glowing again.

A desire sprung up to visit Denny and Genevieve in Paris. I felt embarrassed about having never visited a foreign country, so I wanted to go in order to tell people I'd been there.

After putting off visiting the chapel for a few weeks, I finally agreed to go with Robbie. It was a square-shaped, flat-roofed building of modern design surrounded by apartments on one side and a busy fire station on the other. The congregation consisted of a handful of old ladies plus a few oddbods scattered about.

We were greeted warmly, though I would have preferred to remain anonymous. Never had I felt so uncomfortably out of place sitting there dressed in my combat jacket and jeans.

I couldn't remember a word of the service, such was the discomfort of trying to make it to the end. At the close my escape was blocked by slow-moving people who shook my hand, wishing me well, with smiles from ear to ear. What a relief to hit the pavement and breathe fresh air! I felt exhausted.

During the following week the pastor, Peter McGrath, visited me and we both had a good laugh. He was an ex-docker who'd been in Borstal himself as a lad. He now worked for the Seamen's Mission among the dockers, sailors and prostitutes along Merseyside's lengthy waterfront. He was a down-to-earth character who'd been transformed into one of the nicest men you could ever wish to meet.

It was the warmth of Peter and his wife, Sheila, along with the genuine care of the others that drew me to visit the church again the following week. There was something very real about these people that cut across the age and culture gap between us.

In Peter I found an example I could model myself on over the coming years. His personality contained the graciousness, love and kindness I clearly lacked. He tailored the meetings to suit my limited understanding, spoon-feeding my hunger for knowledge week by week.

After a few months the old ladies kindly suggested I might like to try a bigger church with more young people in case I became bored.

'To be honest,' I answered, 'I've had enough of young people. I just want to know what this Christian life's all about.'

A large part of me accepted that there were no shortcuts on the road to working out my salvation. This was a rugged hands-on apprenticeship where mistakes had to be made.

Before long, I got involved in visiting homes on the estate; it was a rough place that frightened me each time we ventured out. Unemployment was very high. A sense of hopelessness prevailed. Young kids ran wild, gangs roamed at night, the police were always busy and heavy drugs were rampant. Many times our windows were smashed while we sat in a meeting; we were regularly burgled, and visitors often had their cars vandalised.

Fortunately, I'd got to know members of the local gang on the course with Drake Fellowship Centre. They knew that, despite my wishing to pursue my faith, I was no mug. My having been to prison a few times for violence gave me a degree of credibility. If any of them were present when trouble flared at least I had somebody to appeal to.

Some nights when walking home I unwittingly found my path blocked by a crowd hanging around the street corner. It wasn't a good thing having to walk through them, but it was great to hear from their midst: 'All right, Jimmy.'

Being accepted by one of them often meant acceptance by them all. If one of them said I was OK, I'd be left alone.

During that dark winter, two ships sailed into the docks. They were to brighten our lives considerably over two memorable weeks. *Logos* and *Doulos* were crewed by hundreds of young Christians from all over the world, and they belonged to Operation Mobilisation, an international Christian group.

These ships called at ports across the globe, the people then venturing out into the local communities to spread the good news about Jesus. Many of their stories were like mine—rescued by God from prison, drug addiction, prostitution, slavery or war. I visited the ships after college each night to enjoy their fabulous meetings.

During their stay an appeal was made for young believers to join the ship for a two-year stint. I wasted no time in collecting the application forms. This was the best offer I'd heard in years.

On my frequent visits I became friendly with Mario, a young man of my own age from Guatemala in Central America. He'd become a Christian after being put in jail for drug offences—and what a conversion! He now spent his life helping others.

Mario brought people from various nations to visit us at our house each day. We loved their company. They sat watching snooker on TV with fascinated expressions, which was even more fascinating to us, considering the set was only black-and-white!

After 10 days the application forms for joining the ship remained incomplete on a shelf in my room. An apathy seemed to have set in regarding them.

When next I saw Peter, the pastor, I mentioned it to him.

'Hey, Peter, I'd love to sail on one of those ships. I've got the application forms but I just couldn't be bothered filling them in. I don't know what's up with me.'

After a pause he asked in his genial way: 'Do you think God may be telling you to stay, Jim?'

The idea annoyed me immediately. I didn't want God interfering with my plans. Being stopped from anything was always sure to get my back up. Yet beneath my reaction there was no denying that something inside me was reluctant in a big way.

'I'm not trying to tell you what God's saying to you, Jimmy, but you need to consider whether he's telling you to go or not.'

When examining my motives, the reasons for going seemed to lack substance. Travelling the world would give me something to show off about and stick two fingers up to a prison system that had failed to destroy my desire to live. The other motive was to live my Christian life within the cocoon of that loving Christian organisation and be shielded from the reality down on the street.

Within days I realised that neither of these desires would be fulfilled. It was a disappointment.

The final day of the ships' visit arrived quickly and, before I knew it, Mario and I had embraced for the last time in farewell. That night as I lay in bed thinking, I remembered how sad Mario had become one day when I played some music on my hi-fi system. He said it'd reminded him of home.

'Why didn't I give him the tapes?' I thought to myself. 'Get up and do it now, you lazy thing.'

Outside, strong winds drove rain in sheets across the freezing town. I didn't fancy the idea.

'Jesus' disciples would have done it,' came another prodding thought. 'Come on,' I said to myself, pulling back my cosy sheets. 'Let's do it.'

Slates were being blown from house roofs as I ran across the shiny pavements to the docks. The ship lay unguarded. I sneaked on board to search for Mario's cabin. After finding it, I pushed his door open but was halted by his room mate, a Dutchman, who shushed me quiet.

'What do you want?' he whispered. 'Don't wake Mario. He has to be up very early.'

I told him about the tapes and left them on their little table. It would have been nice to hand them to Mario in person, but to do it in secret seemed more appropriate. I went home feeling good.

The following day it was back to the grindstone, working hard in class. We had lots of homework to get through that night so, after supper, I sat watching the news by the fire, preparing myself to start. There was a knock at the door and Robbie went to answer it.

He shouted through: 'There's a surprise here for you, Jimmy.'

I thought he was joking and kept my eye on the TV, but when I looked up, there was Mario standing in the doorway.

'It was too windy to sail,' he said, smiling. 'We'll try tomorrow.'

What a joy to see him again! As usual, he'd brought a companion. David Fox was an oldish man from Ohio in the USA who, being short, looked almost round in a big sheepskin coat. We chatted in my room for a while before having a short time of prayer together before their departure.

When we opened our eyes after praying, David was in tears. He'd seen a vision of something powerful descend on me. The vision had struck him to the core. David left me his address, and we struck up a friendship that would support me through many times of trouble, a friendship that continues to this very day.

It was sad for Robbie and me to see those ships sail out. They'd been an inspirational breath of fresh air to both of us.

'Wouldn't it be great to go with them for a couple of years?' Robbie said later over a cup of tea. 'We could go to the meetings, get all that help, then come back here and have it worked out.'

I knew what he meant. Life was hard and we, as young believing Christians, were constantly tripping up in our faith like kids learning to walk. We both enjoyed the occasional night on the beer, smoking, and a flutter on the horses each Saturday.

'I don't think it's like that, Robbie. If you're willing to learn, God'll teach you everything right within these streets.'

As the words left my mouth, I knew I'd said something really prophetic. A voice immediately seemed to speak within my head: 'And that's how it'll be for you, Jimmy.'

In that moment God was revealing the challenge of his plan for my life over the coming years. The college of my personal training would be those rugged downtown streets of Birkenhead.

In one sense it was a thrill, the kind of crazy struggle people are apt to take on. But in another sense I was deeply disappointed. Gone were the dreams of travelling the world, chasing the sun, completing a degree in a fancy college and living life on Easy Street. Reality told me this was the way it had to be.

There was no use kidding myself. I was a rough diamond that needed cutting into shape. Robbie wondered why I suddenly left the room but such was the weight of the realisation unfolding before me I needed to sit alone and think.

'Has it been real?' I asked myself. 'Can God *really* speak to me through my own mouth?'

As the months leading up to my exams passed by, I gave the prophesy less thought. I waited for things to develop, hoping that God would somehow change his mind.

7
Rocky road to love

During that time I kept up my visits to the staff and young people at the Drake Fellowship Centre. Some courses included young people from Derbyshire who were recruited from a youth cafe in Chesterfield called The Wall.

One day, as I sat on a table in the office, a girl appeared near the door looking out of place. Remembering the discomfort of my own first day, I tried to make conversation by asking whether she was on the present course and where she came from.

Her single-syllable answers suggested she wasn't interested so I gave it a miss. But somehow she stayed on my mind.

My proposed trip to Paris was made all the more possible by the purchase of a 10-year passport. I'd never had a passport before and I felt excited about using it, but deep inside me there was trouble. The desire to go conflicted with an inner knowledge that I shouldn't.

Going abroad was important for my personal credibility. Everybody else travelled, so why shouldn't I? The message to stay within those streets seemed only to fuel my desire to get away.

I turned my attention to the exams and left the Paris issue for another day. I felt satisfied that, no matter what my results, I'd worked hard and revised well.

In the event, I managed an 'A' grade in English and reasonable results in maths and sociology. A year had elapsed since my release from prison. I felt good about the way things had gone. The weather was warming up again, a long summer break was in store and I'd kept myself in good physical shape.

At the Drake Centre I was offered a place on a bridge-building project up in the Scottish Highlands. I wasn't terribly keen until a name on the list caught my eye: Joanne Riley from Derbyshire. I felt sure it was the same girl who'd snubbed me some months before so, out of roguish curiosity, I agreed to go.

Thinking of her reminded me of how much I missed having a girlfriend. The few liaisons I'd experienced since release had all led up the wrong path. I'd even begun praying to God to find a wife for me.

The course objective was to build a bridge across a small river that would enable the foresters to avoid a massive detour during the winter, when the river was in flood.

On the day the course started, 12 of us turned up in dribs and drabs carrying an assortment of bags, cameras and Walkmans. The centre looked as if a bomb had hit it as we moved kit from the stores into the trailer.

Joanne Riley was indeed the girl I'd spoken to previously and, thankfully, on this occasion she was more relaxed and willing to talk. She was the only girl on the course, and as soon as we hit the road, a contest for her attention began in earnest. I kept myself in the background, not wanting to make my attraction towards her so blatantly obvious as the others seemed to be doing.

The journey, though scenic, grew increasingly boring as darkness fell and the clock ticked by. But after 10½ hours we pulled into a tiny forestry village on the outskirts of a little place called Taynuilt.

Desmond, the ranger, greeted us and invited the whole crew into the living room of his warm cottage. He soon had us making stacks of toast, sipping a 'wee dram' of whisky and guzzling mugs of tea. His Springer Spaniel slept in front of the log fire and, as our eyes glistened in the flickering light, we wondered what manner of man he was to live without a TV. Never had we heard of such behaviour!

Desmond was a bright-eyed, straight-talking man who took a personal interest in everybody, explained things thoroughly and expected people to work as hard as he did. Later, we moved to the cowshed we were staying in and tried to get some sleep. However, the midges had other ideas and began biting my poor English legs. I was up half the night scratching.

In the morning we split into groups to start a variety of tasks—cutting wood, shovelling stones for cement, rustproofing girders, digging banks and preparing meals. The rain drizzled on us for three days, making conditions difficult and extremely muddy, but everybody worked hard regardless.

In the evenings we swam in the lochs, played *shinty* (wild Scottish hockey) and learned how to fire a shotgun. I enjoyed making Joanne laugh when we were together and began enjoying her company more each day.

At one stage, Desmond asked me to assist her make a hollow wooden box that, when filled with cement, would form the pillars on which the bridge would stand. I deliberately let her make the box the wrong shape in order to spend more time with her correcting it. Desmond couldn't understand how we'd made such an elementary mistake!

After working flat out for four days we were given a well-earned break in Oban, a harbour town. We got up early, washing, cleaning hair, shaving and trying to look smart in the creased clothes we pulled from our bags. Arriving in Oban we made a beeline for the nearest pub and, within minutes, the juke box was playing, pints were being pulled, cigarettes lit and balls lined up on the pool table.

I noticed Joanne didn't seem to be enjoying it, and I wanted to ask her out for a walk. But I felt afraid of being rejected. Instead, I took a gamble by rising to my feet and saying within her earshot: 'Blow this for a lark. I'm off for a walk.'

As I took the first step towards the door, I hoped upon hope that she'd come with me. If she didn't, I'd be out on the street alone, having blown a good opportunity.

'Can I walk along with you?' came the magic words. I couldn't believe my luck.

'Yeah, come on,' I said casually, trying to stay cool.

The only problem now might be if somebody else wanted to come with us. I figured on their being held back by the drink, and I was right. Suddenly, we were out on the pavement submerging into the busy streets of the lively tourist town. We wandered around talking about everything.

The best part was spent overlooking the beautiful bay from

McCaig's Tower, situated high above the town. It was up there that I began to fall for this Joanne Riley, and so began the painful turmoil of love. The time spent alone with her did nothing to satisfy my desire to be with her. Instead, it increased it to a terrible ache.

Over the next couple of days I treasured every moment of her company, making her laugh, helping her out and trying to act smart. She had to leave for home two days before the end of the course and, for my own sake, I was glad to see her go. It'd be easier with her completely out of sight than so tantalisingly close.

I'd never felt this way before—pain mixed with joy, happiness with sadness, brightness with raging darkness. My emotions were out of control. In fear of my own feelings I'd kept them well hidden, but there was no disguising my delight when Joanne suggested we exchange addresses and keep in touch.

But what was I thinking about? She had a steady boyfriend who had money, she lived miles away in Derbyshire and, in reality, she'd soon forget somebody like me.

As the course drew to a close with the successful completion of the bridge, we returned to Merseyside and dispersed to our respective homes.

No sooner had I arrived back at the house than my desire to visit Paris raised its head again. I avoided discussing the issue with Peter, my pastor, for fear of it becoming obvious that I shouldn't go. I wanted circumstances to carry me helplessly along, but the decision-making process was firmly in my court. Responsibility was mine no matter how hard I tried to wriggle out of it.

The fact that I'd already told people I was going to Paris made it harder to turn back. My pride wouldn't allow it. I didn't want to be all talk and no action. While out shopping one afternoon I pushed all doubts to the back of my mind and bought a return ticket. I wasn't used to obeying an inner voice, and it annoyed me having to wrestle with it so vigorously. I'd be glad to go and be done with it.

After travelling to London by early-morning bus, I caught another bus to Dover with a group of holidaymakers and took the hovercraft to Calais. Once through customs I continued by rail across country to my destination.

Genevieve had agreed to meet me in a small cafe near the Gare de Lyon. After finding the place quite easily, ordering a coffee and ringing Genevieve's office, I sat and waited. Within an hour we were together, feeling quite strange at seeing each other again. She seemed quite distracted, as if I'd arrived at an awkward time. But once we'd eaten a good meal in her apartment, the atmosphere seemed more relaxed.

I'd avoided alcohol for a few months, but when Genevieve produced a bottle of champagne I allowed myself the indulgence. In letting it pass down my throat I was deliberately weakening my resolve—one drink would inevitably lead to another—but I did it regardless, pushing God out of the way completely.

Each night we ventured out on to the busy streets, visiting bars and theatres, playing pinball, eating meals with friends and having fun. I knew Genevieve had fallen for me but she held herself back, wrestling with something unseen. During the day, while she worked, I travelled all over the city, visiting the sights, jogging around parks and meeting up with Denny.

Seeing him again wasn't as exciting as I'd expected. He was busy getting on with his life and a certain spark had gone from our friendship. In an effort to relive something of the past, I spent an afternoon drinking with him in an Arab bar near the Arc de Triomph. We had lots of fun thrashing two Germans on the pinball machine. The owners weren't used to people clocking up free games so regularly.

As the afternoon wore on, Denny became increasingly abusive to those around us, acting more outrageous with each drink that passed his lips. It was obviously a rough establishment where injury could easily result without much fuss. But Denny was in his element, turning his back on the Arabs to play pinball after fanning their anger into a fury.

At the point where things were about to explode, I managed to hold the Arabs back long enough to persuade an obstinate Denny to leave. It was a horrible reminder of a life I could never return to, living on the edge of danger and trouble.

That night we stayed at his apartment across the city. As he slept, I sat looking out at the Parisian skyline, convinced that I had to return home. I'd come here and been neither the reformed believer nor the wild man of old, falling instead into a grey wasteland of obscurity and emptiness. I stood for nothing, a hypocrite of both camps, without dignity or character. Oh, God! What a mess I'd made!

The last couple of days with Genevieve were equally as difficult, her uncertainties rising up into annoyance. It was a good thing I was leaving. She, like Denny, knew more than I did the depth of my conversion to Christ and its effect on our friendship.

She'd fallen in love with me but knew it could never be. Allowing herself into a relationship now would only lead to an inevitable split in the near future. The pain wasn't worth it. A relationship needs hope, and with me there could be none.

At the train station awaiting departure, I stood with her, feeling like an empty fool. Instead of speaking openly about what was really happening, I acted as if everything was all right.

As my train pulled in, I said, 'Goodbye, Gen. I'd better go.'

I leaned forward to kiss her cheek but she pulled back.

'Go home to your God!' she snapped.

I stood there feeling stupid and looked at her sheepishly.

'Just go!' she said again.

I walked towards the gate feeling hurt and embarrassed. It was the end for us, an unhappy conclusion. The leanness that had filled my being from the outset of this excursion became a dull ache weighing heavily on me all the way home.

Having deliberately ignored the God who'd set me free, I now felt hurt and ashamed. The least I could do was learn something from the experience. The lessons were plain to see. God's warning voice had been so gentle. It had been easy to ignore him and carry on. His law was written on my heart. I knew the boundary lines but wasn't used to knuckling down. I'd wanted to be swept along by a wave of circumstance that would leave me looking innocent, but there could be no shifting of blame; it belonged to me.

It was a tough deal compared with my past life. In those days my daily hope was to fall upon tasty situations in which to indulge, but now those days were gone. While professing to know God I'd have to be accountable for my actions every single day. It seemed unfair that all around me people were able to do anything they pleased. But in truth I knew their freedom was an illusion—I'd lived their kind of life and knew its emptiness.

In an effort to clean up my conscience I attended all the chapel services, even punishing myself in an act of penitence by joining in the most boring of them. But no matter how hard I tried, the guilt clung like a leech.

On one particular afternoon, after two weeks of struggling, I knelt down in my room determined to pray freely. But those familiar clouds of guilt and unworthiness gathered around me again.

In frustration, I sprang to my feet, tired of being pushed down, and began spitting out angry words while poking the air with an accusing finger.

'Devil! I know you're here. I'm *sick* of you trying to push me down. I *hate* you. You've tried to ruin my life right from the start. You loved it when my family were brokenhearted because of my imprisonment. You laugh when people choke themselves on the things you tempt them with.

'Well, I'm getting back on my feet. I'm a fighter who'll never stay down. No matter how many times you knock me down I'll get back up. There'll never be a day when you can forget about me. I'll keep trying to win people over from your evil clutches.

'You're trying to pile the guilt on me so I'll be ineffective. But it won't work because I *know* that, through Jesus Christ, I'm forgiven—I'm set free. It's a fact that you can't change—that's why you have to lie. *So get out! Go!*'

As I fell back to my knees, the heaviness lifted completely. It left a lightness I hadn't felt for weeks, and I began to pray easily.

Just as I was ending the prayer, a voice said: 'Go to the office.' It wasn't audible—neither a feeling nor a thought, but a clear message. I didn't know how seriously to take it but decided to ride up to Pat's office in Laird Street anyway.

Unfortunately, when I got there they told me he'd gone out. I made my way back down to Conway Street and visited the Drake Centre instead. As usual, the big office was busy with phones ringing, everybody talking and people coming and going. I sat near the door minding my own business, but when I looked at Dougie I noticed he was staring at me with a curious expression.

'John, is Judy still on the payroll?' he asked the bookkeeper.

While John checked in his books Dougie rose to his feet and kept up his strange stare at me.

'No, she's finished now, Doug,' John finally said.

By this time I began feeling uncomfortable under his gaze. I was about to leave when he suddenly spoke to me.

'Do you want a job, son?'

I was shocked. People turned to see what was happening.

'Well, yes. Is it a proper job?'

'Yes,' he said, still staring, with hands in pockets, from behind his desk.

'Not a government scheme?'

'Nope.'

'A proper instructor's job?'

'Yep.'

'Wow, thanks, Dougie. When will it start?'

'Today, son. You're working for me right now. You can spend the afternoon helping out.'

Suddenly, I felt claustrophobic. I wanted to be an instructor but not this afternoon. I needed space to breathe. The freedom I'd enjoyed while unemployed was suddenly being cut off and I was going to miss it.

'But I've got to do some things this afternoon,' I lied. 'I didn't expect to be working and it's caught me on the hop.'

'What things have you got to do?' he asked bluntly.

'Well—er—just things, Doug. You know.' I was struggling. The need to get out heightened.

'OK,' he said after a pause. 'Let's have you in here at nine in the morning.'

'All right, thanks,' I said. 'See ya tomorrow.'

I left without looking as if I was in a hurry. Once outside I bombed it around the streets on my bike with my head in a whirl. Despite the thrill of getting this particularly exciting job I needed the afternoon to gather my thoughts and prepare myself.

That evening I phoned my family, members of the chapel and some friends to let them know the good news. When I was asked my level of pay, working hours and conditions of employment, I didn't know a thing!

The day had been eventful. Before going to bed I remembered the confrontation with the devil and the voice that followed, instructing me to 'go to the office'. It was incredible to think that God would actively speak and move on my behalf. Like a true parent he wanted me to grow and flourish in this world, but I'd have to listen; the choice was mine.

Back into my mind came the unpopular message spoken after the ships had left: 'within these streets'. This job was a piece in the jigsaw God was fitting together; his awesome power seemed very close. He'd worked against the odds. I was an ex-convict with a bad record, hardly any work experience, few educational qualifications, living in an unemployment black spot, getting a great job in a depressed part of a depressed town.

This was the launchpad from which my potential would be drawn out and developed, a job in which I'd face up to some hard facts about life. It was also one in which I'd become a man.

8
Joanne

I moved out from Stonham's into a friend's apartment on the estate behind our street. Staying at Mark's place would be a lot cheaper, which was important now I was working for money.

Mark was part Afro-Caribbean, loved his Reggae music, wore a permanent smile and stayed up each night making disco speakers from old cupboards and drawers. The apartments were situated in a rough area with no shortage of incidents, but I spent most of my time away on the job.

Work itself began with two trips to the Lake District taking difficult groups in glorious summer conditions. My team leader was Arthur, a nutcase ex-paratrooper who needed to be controlled as much as the course scallywags! He and I got on fine and we shared a lot of laughs.

After a few weeks I was handed a payslip for £350; I'd forgotten all about wages and received more than expected. Kenny, my fellow instructor, had to help me open a bank account to pay the cheque into, something I'd never done before. It was embarrassing having such limited experience of everyday living like this—another legacy of a misspent youth.

Working for the Drake Centre meant I got a free ride on all the best trips. This was to include a forthcoming canoe expedition. Joanne Riley was due to join—we'd kept in touch since Scotland. I was thrilled when she accepted my invitation to come over a couple of days early in order to let me show her around Merseyside.

I met her off the train at Liverpool's Lime Street Station. She looked great and seemed as pleased to see me as I was to see her. After a quick bite to eat we set off for the movies to catch *Indiana Jones*, where we had great fun. It felt great having a good-looking female companion with whom I could share some decent conversation.

During the show I wanted to put my arm around her or give her a kiss but felt too afraid—my nerves were on edge. Later, while waiting at the bus stop, I somehow managed to pluck up enough courage to kiss her. Our embrace was mutual; we were glad to be together.

During the ride back, our conversation grew more intimate and I was able to share how I'd fallen for her in Scotland. She laughed in surprise. Having Joanne as a girlfriend sent me bursting with pride. I walked with a skip in my step, and I smiled from ear to ear.

On the canoe trip it was hard to keep my distance from her. Arthur was in his element, singing lullabies, making fun of us day and night.

Something I hadn't bargained for was the emergence of underlying insecurities that bubbled up alongside the love I felt for Joanne. I usually liked to keep my feelings well under control but Joanne, by her very presence, could drag them all up. It was a tiresome battle trying to wrestle with jealousy, desire, rejection, possessiveness and passion.

Despite the heartache of putting her back on the train to Derbyshire afterwards, in some ways I was glad to see Joanne go. At least life would become a little less complicated. When she arrived home, Joanne learnt she'd been accepted at a college in Wrexham to do a degree in youth and community. This was good news for Joanne, and it brought her within visiting distance of me. We often met halfway, in the city of Chester, for a day out.

I was having to take my job a little more seriously. The weather was getting colder, the courses were more difficult and the team leader needed better support. It stung me to be told off by Dougie for coming in a few minutes late each morning.

Soon after this, I was questioned about my attitude, which they said had deteriorated. Their criticism hurt my feelings, making me defensive and angry. I wasn't used to being open to knocks. But despite the difficulty of the situation, I managed to accept their words and pledged to make a greater effort.

The truth was, my mind had become so filled with Joanne, I seemed to be neglecting the young people I was working with. This set me thinking about my relationship with her. I loved her but wondered whether we seriously had a future.

Since moving to Mark's apartment, beginning work and going out with Joanne, my faith had begun to slide again. Joanne knew about my beliefs and admired me for them. But she'd expressed her view about them using lines from a Shakespeare play that described an attractive flower containing a poison.

Unless Joanne became a believer like me, a struggle would always exist between us—her pulling me in one direction or me pulling her in another. The painful memory of my experience with Genevieve and the stupid way in which I'd allowed it all to happen was still fresh in my mind.

The true fulfilment of my life lay in my walk with the God who'd saved me. No matter how much I desired Joanne, the price of losing my way along the path was too high to pay. With these thoughts in mind I decided my relationship with Joanne must come to an end.

What a painful encounter lay ahead! My heart, which had become so intimately attached to her, now had to be torn away. How had I allowed myself to be lured down this path? Why did I have to go on making the same mistakes over and over again?

'What an absolute fool I am—no strength and unable to stand by my own word!' I felt angry with this Christian life. Having constantly to dig myself out of a mess was a tiresome business. But my mind was made up. The next time we were together, I'd finish the relationship.

Joanne could sense that something was afoot the next time we were together at Mark's apartment. She seemed almost ready for what was about to take place. We exchanged small talk for a short time before I fell into my own thoughts while she pottered around in the kitchen.

'Hey, God,' I thought, 'I hope you realise how much this is gonna hurt me. You're either gonna have to give me a wife or take away my desires.'

I felt annoyed.

'I suppose the only way this could work out is if Joanne got saved like me,' I mused. But another thought jumped up to say,

'Yes, but that's just selfish, Jimmy, something to suit you.'

'No, it isn't,' I countered. 'I want Joanne to become a Christian even if I never see her again—for her own sake.'

Joanne came back into the room to continue our conversation, but this time she seemed more serious, almost lost in her own thoughts. She was talking about Shakespeare again, the battle between good and bad, darkness and light, right and wrong. Tears formed in her eyes, her lip quivered as she tried to talk and then great sobs broke out.

Joanne was kneeling on the floor, speaking to God through tears! Only then did I begin to realise what was happening. I remember seeing my own tears fall into her hair as she went through this incredible experience. It was a moment I'll never forget.

I'd shared my own experience of God with her but never expected this kind of outcome. Unlike many people I've since seen receiving Jesus Christ, Joanne came through feeling angry. She was an independent kind of girl who made her own decisions without reference to God or the devil.

Joanne liked to think she existed in a grey area between good and bad, but on this day she realised that no grey area existed. People were either in one camp or the other. The anger came from realising she'd never *really* been independent but had been manipulated by a force outside her understanding.

The Bible says that the devil has 'blinded the minds of unbelievers'. An unbeliever needs to realise who's pulling his strings!

Now Joanne was a Christian. It took days for it fully to sink into my mind. I felt so proud taking her to the mission. I asked her to marry me shortly after; no sooner had she accepted than I began questioning whether it was God's will for us. Poor Joanne couldn't have known quite what was happening!

She returned to college pledging to pray about it, while I went back to work to do the same. Joanne quickly found some Christian students who met regularly and supported each other well. At work, the honeymoon period was over for me. I was having to learn how to handle tough troupes, run rock-climbing and abseiling sessions, organise kayaking trips and lead general mountaineering.

The onset of winter meant I had to spend hundreds of pounds on equipment. Dougie also reminded me of the need to gain a driving licence, and almost two months of my pay was spent on a series of driving lessons. For a few months the job cost me more than I was being paid, but the expenditure seemed a good investment. Having no driving licence was yet another annoying legacy of my past; it seemed I was constantly rebuilding and catching up on things I'd neglected.

During my walk into work in the mornings an element introduced itself into my routine that helped lift the blues whenever I felt down. Up ahead a bus would appear on the flyover and slowly snake its way through the rush-hour traffic to pass by. Nobody took much notice of it on those cold mornings, but I knew those men in the middle section were all handcuffed together. It was the Risley bus! Prison officers were transporting prisoners to court from that notorious remand centre where, in the past, I'd suffered so much pain.

The men would be enjoying their anonymous trip through the streets, keeping an eye open for familiar faces and attractive women before being locked beneath the courts for the day. They'd have been brought from their cells early in the morning to be herded into that ugly cage in the reception area. Then they'd had to get changed into musty-smelling clothes and been given a pitiful breakfast. I knew the look in their eyes and the ache in their hearts as they passed me by. It was a good stick from which to measure how far I'd come since those mean old days.

On Joanne's next visit we talked further about getting married but still had no concrete answers to our prayers. My expectations were full to bursting-point. I hoped the answer would flash up like a neon light saying 'Yes' or 'No'.

It was while I was strolling among shoppers later in the day that a vision suddenly came to me of an old table-top filled with odds and ends. The whole thing seemed to represent the reality of Joanne and marriage, as opposed to the rose-coloured one I hoped for.

After I glanced at it briefly, it lifted out of sight.

Joanne walked beside me, oblivious to what was happening. I wanted to see it again and, as though connected to my thoughts, it came back. The picture suggested that our marriage would be a long struggle, something we'd have to fight for and work at. It certainly set me thinking twice about the whole thing. But before making up my mind I just had to see it one last time. Down it came again, this time briefly but long enough for me to understand its meaning.

I paused in the street to think; into my mind came my hero, King David of Israel. His whole life had been a struggle but, with God, he continually overcame. 'With God I can do it,' I said to myself.

'Come on, Jo, that's it. We're getting married.'

'But what's happened? Why suddenly . . . ?' She looked really surprised.

'God's given me the choice,' I said, 'and I choose to.'

We made our way happily to a nice jeweller's and I bought Joanne the ring she liked best. I kept it in my pocket until we got to a pizza parlour for lunch, where I could present it to her properly. After we'd ordered, I took it out, looked straight into her eyes and placed the ring on her finger.

The waitress returned, looking glassy-eyed, and asked tentatively: 'Have you just—er—you know, got engaged?'

'Yes,' we said together, smiling.

'Oh, isn't it lovely?' she said. 'Another couple did it in here last week. I wish my fella'd hurry up!'

We laughed as she walked away, feeling like the two luckiest people in the world.

Shortly after this I failed my driving test. It was a nerve-racking experience that I thoroughly hated. But I didn't worry too much, knowing I'd pass sooner or later.

Dougie saw things differently. He warned that if I didn't pass soon I'd be out of a job since driving the minibuses was supposed to be a major part of my work. It shocked me to be given such an ultimatum, as for some reason I thought my position was watertight.

The minimum time for retesting was a month, so I applied straightaway and booked more lessons to fill the gap. Our storeman, Rossi, was in the same predicament, but unfortunately he failed his test and was asked to leave, which really turned up the heat.

Joanne and I couldn't see the point in having a long, drawn-out engagement. We wanted to be married within four months. In making our enquiries we discovered that the mission wasn't registered to perform weddings so we'd have to marry legally at the registry office, then have the blessing of a church service separately. Finding a place to live would be the next job; it made sense to buy a little place on a 100 per cent mortgage, the repayments being cheaper than paying rent.

The numerous estate agents had plenty of properties to throw at us, but we soon became bored with the tiresome business of making appointments and viewing. We looked at fewer and fewer until after a while neither of us was doing anything.

Feeling guilty about my apathetic approach, I ventured out alone on my bike one afternoon for another look. Once again, I soon lost interest and found myself taking a shortcut back through the estate to the apartment. On my way down Paterson Street a nice little end-terrace house caught my eye. It wasn't for sale but I rode in a circle looking at it.

'That type of house'd suit us fine,' I thought.

During Joanne's next visit we agreed to try looking again. Despite praying to God for help, we still had to get our skates on and do something. While walking through town we called at the first estate agent's we came across.

As we closed the door behind us, the lady at the desk spoke up with enthusiasm. 'Hello. I think I've got just the thing for a young couple like you.'

I didn't like people telling me what I liked. But when I saw the photograph attached to the document she'd laid on the counter, my interest was aroused immediately. There before me was a picture of the little end-terrace I'd looked on with fondness only a week before.

'What do you think?' the lady asked.

Something drew me warmly to this house; it was more than a coincidence to be offered it in this way.

'Is this house at the bottom end of Paterson Street?' I asked to make sure.

'Yes, it is,' she answered.

'What do you think, Jimmy?' asked Joanne. 'Worth a visit?'

'We don't need to visit—I *know* it's the house for us.'

'You can't just make an offer without even *looking* at it,' said Joanne, staring at me as if I was crazy.

'OK, we'll look. But I feel sure.'

Once outside, I was able to tell Joanne about the sequence of events that had led us to view this particular house. With each step I was becoming more convinced that God was manoeuvring on our behalf in order to shape our immediate future.

Back into my mind came the message, 'Within these streets', and the subsequent, 'Go to the office', that led to the job. Then I recalled Joanne's amazing salvation and the visions about our marriage; everything was falling into place.

After taking a look at the house, we made an offer and began what seemed to us the complicated matter of getting a mortgage. The agency told us to expect the keys within a couple of months, maybe sooner.

It was pleasing to have that hurdle out of the way but, before we knew it, the final obstacle presented itself—my driving test. The pressure on me was tremendous. Everything suddenly hinged on whether I passed or failed. No licence meant no job, which in turn meant no house or wedding. Everything could collapse!

During the run-up to the driving test my nerves were shot. I kept imagining making stupid mistakes and failing again. It was a nightmare.

While I was praying with Joanne during this time of worry, my attention was drawn to Jeremiah 17:9 in the Good News Bible: 'Who can understand the human heart? There is nothing else so deceitful; it is too sick to be healed.'

As I considered what this meant, it occurred to me that it was my *heart* that was causing all the trouble by coming up with all sorts of negative scenarios. My *mind* knew that I'd completed all the driving manoeuvres perfectly well on numerous occasions and that I was fully capable of passing the test. I therefore rejected the lies of my heart and took firm hold of the facts in my mind.

It was a positive experience that helped send me off with an air of confidence the following morning. Thankfully, the examiner, unlike the previous one, seemed quite amiable and even managed a smile. I got off to a good start, running through the gears smoothly, manoeuvring the car with composure and keeping my eye on the dreaded rear-view mirror.

When, after five minutes, I noticed him taking more notice of the women out walking than of my driving, I knew I was on to a winner. But at the end, despite completing what I thought was a good test, it was impossible to tell whether I'd passed or failed.

After scribbling in his pad, he turned to me and said, 'Mr Rice, I'm pleased to say you've passed your test.'

I couldn't believe my ears! I could have kissed the man and run a lap of honour around Birkenhead! The relief was incredible. I could hardly wait to get back and tell Joanne.

When I arrived, she was leaning over the verandah looking down on to the street, waiting. I tried to remain straight-faced in order to keep her guessing, but as our eyes met, the joy came out in a big smile and, with clenched fists raised in triumph, I said, *'I've done it, Jo!'*

I wasn't likely to forget in a hurry that special word from the Bible. That ancient book was reaching across the ages to help me again.

I had to catch a train to South Wales in order to join up with the team who were working with a group in the Brecon Beacons. Before boarding, I phoned Dougie to thank him for kicking my backside into gear concerning my attitude towards the job, which in turn had pushed me through the driving test. He was very pleased I'd passed.

After a few trips to South Wales, I returned with the worst bout of flu I'd ever had, putting me in bed for over a week. It was highly frustrating being laid up. Nothing normally held me back at all; my middle name was energy. During that endless week of shivering sweat, drinking bottles of Lucozade and eating tubs of ice cream, I also grew impatient with our wedding arrangements. The keys to the house were due to be handed over within a couple of weeks, and I wanted us to have the registry office side of things completed quickly so we could move in. I asked Joanne to go ahead and book the first available date.

My action showed what little concept I had of family expectations, how much others would like to have been involved or how traditional they may have wished things to be. When I think back, there were faint voices, such as Peter and Sheila, trying to slow me down. But I had a headstrong personality and did things *my* way. To me, the formalities were obstacles that needed to be overcome, nuisances blocking my path.

On Valentine's Day 1985, we entered the registry office with a small band of witnesses and quietly sealed the marriage.

It was an exciting day in itself, but when we returned to Mark's apartment and sat on the edge of the bed, we felt completely deflated. The enormity of our actions began to sink in, the weight of them creating a feeling of isolation and vulnerability.

My nature was to push things hard, whether they be physical exercise, studying or my faith. On this occasion, my actions had left us floating adrift and I felt sorry for Joanne. It was a clear indication of my need to harness my untamed nature and take responsibility in thinking for two instead of one.

After two weeks, we visited the solicitor to collect the keys for the house. It was a real thrill for us to get them. I'd borrowed a van from work in order for us to move in straightaway. Our few possessions were unable to fill the back of the small minibus; besides our clothes we had a bed, lamp, toastmaker, kettle, radio cassette and desk.

Despite being a small, two-bedroomed terrace it still looked fairly empty after we moved in. We borrowed a table and some chairs from the mission, but we still had to buy toiletries, curtains, carpets and a cooker. We also had to have the gas switched on and a phone installed.

It was a nightmare of complications, the likes of which I'd never tackled before. I was useless at putting up curtain rails or repairing things, often throwing everything to the floor in exasperation. Joanne was beginning to realise just who she'd married.

Money had to be put aside for incoming bills, which left us with less than ever. My habit of carrying bundles of it around in cash had to stop when it kept running through my fingers. It was an uncomfortable learning experience where we had to think on our feet.

At work I was having to learn, at home I was having to learn and at church I was having to learn. Being a novice clashed with my pride. I longed for the day when my abilities in all departments were fully developed, but that day seemed a long way off.

The marriage service soon came round, during which we had our union blessed by the pastor and made our vows publicly before God. It was a superb day. A great collection of friends and family joined together in wishing us well, and every chair was filled. We were presented with all sorts of beautiful gifts and cards. Two special guests were Gerry and Annette, who'd travelled all the way up from Grendon.

Afterwards, a whole crowd of folk came back for a look at the house, filling it to the rafters. Their bustling presence sealed a beginning for us in that place; our married life had really begun.

The wedding was arranged to coincide with our Easter break, which enabled us to spend two weeks having fun together. After that, I returned to work and Joanne to college, where she stayed for two nights each week. I missed her on those occasions but thought it important she finish her studies.

Married life had got off to a good start, but little did we realise what traumatic events we'd have to face together.

9
Roller coaster living

With me working away so much, often Joanne returned to an empty house.

One time, she found the place had been burgled. Fear suddenly gripped her; she was alone and vulnerable in a relatively strange, crime-ridden area. Her instinctive reaction was to attempt to contact me through Dougie at the office. But Dougie, being a former Marine with a wife who'd been through plenty of similar experiences, set about calming her down. One of the girls from the office stayed with her overnight, while everybody else kept in close contact during the few days before my return.

Fortunately, the burglar didn't cause any damage. It had been a quick job, with just two pieces of electrical equipment taken, probably the work of a junkie looking for easy money.

It was the first time I'd truly considered Joanne's position of being a long way from home in a town full of strangers. What made things worse was that I was due to be home for only two nights—it was one of those rare occasions when we did two courses back-to-back.

Jo and I stayed close together over that short period. On the morning of my departure I could find no words to comfort her. What *could* I say? We'd bought two sets of stationery with stamps and promised to write each day.

With a full rucksack on my back, I turned to her on the doorstep and said quite crisply, 'I'm sorry, Jo. You *know* I have to go, and because I've got to go, there's nothing I can do to help. Only God can help. If you look to him, he'll deliver you from all this. You must seek him out.'

At this, I crossed the street, disappeared through the alleyway opposite and submerged into the housing estate.

'How have I ended up in this no-win situation?' I asked myself. No reasonable alternatives had been available. I hated having to say what I'd said, but somehow I knew it was right.

It was a thoroughly miserable Jimmy Rice who travelled up to Scotland that day with a particularly rowdy group ready to build another bridge. I sent Jo a card from a motorway service station on the way so that she'd receive something quickly. The real letter-writing began late that night while I sat up in my sleeping-bag leaning against the wall of the large equipment store.

Trying to occupy a dozen street-wise young men that week was difficult enough without the terrible weather conditions that descended on us. We had to abandon the bridge project after three futile days of trying to start. We concentrated instead on other tasks. Some of the group went out culling deer with the ranger while others planted trees, laid paths and undertook a variety of jobs. It was unsatisfying since we couldn't get anything finished. Without the bridge, our time became fragmented.

An important element on these courses was the inclusion of young women. Their presence took the sting out of any bunch of lads and helped to balance proceedings. On this occasion there weren't any, so the jokes grew more dirty, interaction more aggressive and attitudes more bullish.

Quite by accident, a situation arose one evening that knocked the frustration out of us all. Two lads had a wrestling match on the straw-covered concrete floor. They were under the careless eye of a referee, perched on a stack of crates under the dim lights, smoking a cigarette. When they'd finished, two others had a go, followed by two more.

In the midst of the groaning, shouting, sweat and dust, we found ourselves split into two groups, one at either end of the grappling area. Each group took turns in allowing one of their gang to select an opponent from the other. The level of noise was fantastic as each team roared their man on.

It was hilarious how we all adopted the exaggerated behaviour of TV wrestling spectators. We threatened the opposing team with shouts and gestures while the fighters, stripped down to their jeans, rolled and scraped their way around the floor into hay bales and boxes while trying to get the better of each other.

I had five contests, four of them with a big punk called Dave, who looked like a Red Indian and was as strong as an ox. It took a submission or shoulders pin-down to win, but neither of us could get the better of the other. All our fights ended in total exhaustion, with both of us having to crawl from the ring.

After what seemed like hours, we drifted away to flop into our sleeping bags, covered with dust, scrapes, bruises and ripped clothing. But it was the best part of the course, and it served to help us enjoy the remaining few days.

A steady flow of letters began to arrive from Joanne, each filled with the news of how God was standing with her every day. She quoted pieces of the Bible that had almost leapt off the pages as she read them, each containing promises of care and protection. Joanne was making the fantastic discovery that God's Word, the Bible, can be relied on. It may sound crazy, but that old Bible has good news for us today.

The expanse of time that separated me from going home held similar frustrations to those I'd experienced in prison. I wanted to run back to Joanne's rescue and deliver her from all the anxieties, but I became aware of God's hidden hand wanting to do the job himself. His ways often involve isolating people in order to get their attention, or putting on pressure through circumstances to prove his reliability when called upon.

The Joanne I returned to was one who'd taken her first steps into security with God, away from being tossed by the waves of life in meaningless directions. A part of her that had previously relied on me now had its trust in God; although I knew this was true, I felt a bit put out at the time.

As we drifted into another summer, Joanne and I became increasingly involved in the Sunday school run by the old ladies at the mission. Despite their genuine love for the kids, the ladies' strength and health had seen better years and the load had become quite a strain. We bounced on to the scene bringing a youthful enthusiasm, utilising the helpers we recruited. After a few months, the ladies dropped out, leaving it all to us.

Some of the kids filled their Sundays by hopping from one Sunday school to another. It made no difference to them which kind of church they visited.

Many came from homes where they were exposed to high levels of crime and violence, along with alcohol, drugs and other forms of abuse. Most were from unemployed one-parent families who walked a thin line between destitution and manageable debts.

These little ones were receiving a miserable medicine passed down from a disenfranchised generation that had fallen on hopeless times. The sexual adventures of their parents' youth had produced a crop that would undoubtedly bear a similar harvest in time to come.

As the children arrived at the mission each Sunday, a gang of their compatriots arrived to threaten them with violence, pulling some away at the doors, spitting on them as they entered. Older ones clambered all over the roof, hanging down to gesticulate through the windows. Others sneaked in to try to disrupt or cause damage. People living nearby saw what was happening. But fear of retribution forced them into neglect; nobody reported anything. Occasionally it was peaceful, but not often.

The uncertainty began playing on my nerves. Fear rose in me each week as we were about to walk across to the mission. We prayed like mad before leaving the house, but it didn't seem to make any difference. I became really angry with God and told him so.

But the person giving me most trouble was myself. Sunken insecurities were rising to the surface, stirred up by these events. I wanted to run from the problem but had nowhere to go. I'd have to stay put and face it. Talking about these things with the pastor was probably the best idea, but something inside me was averse to letting it out. Instead, it was Joanne who had to listen as I droned on about everyone and everything, keeping the blame far away from myself.

She became exasperated, not knowing how to react or what to suggest. What had happened to the strong, lively Jimmy she'd married? Fear danced around in my guts whenever we went to the mission as I listened for the persecutors to arrive. Others felt annoyed at the disturbances, but nobody else seemed gripped by anxiety as badly as me. The fact that I was very fit and had experienced numerous fights made no difference. The old ladies and the pastor were all much stronger than me. I was the weakest!

Any romantic notions I'd held of following in the valiant footsteps of my heroes recorded in the Bible were now quashed in the light of the pathetic discoveries I was making about myself. Deep inside I knew there was a long way to go before God was finished doing his work within these streets.

Often in life we scatter the gloom of today with bright hopes for the future. One horizon for us was Joanne's being allowed to join me on a trip to the French Pyrenees in late summer.

We'd often talked about visiting the Alps or other big mountain ranges, so the Pyrenees with their peaks doubling the size of anything in Britain was a wish come true. As the trip coincided with Joanne's birthday we agreed it would be her present. (But secretly I bought her a gold chain and kept it hidden in my rucksack.)

Several weeks before departure our team leader resigned. This left Kenny and me to organise things until a suitable replacement could be found. Having to make decisions brought us to a new level of awareness and responsibility.

The Pyrenees group we'd selected for the trip were great fun. Their songs and laughter made the long drive through England and France seem short. We rested at a camp on the edge of Limoges on the way down, before hitting the heart of the Pyrenees the following day.

Our camp was situated beneath a mountain whose peak reached over 10,000 feet. Along the other side ran a big gorge where we had great fun jumping into deep pools and swimming around. A game we played was to follow an instructor as he climbed across the walls above the pools; the penalty for falling was a big, cold splash.

My group decided to take a day off sunbathing before embarking on our main objective: a six-day circular expedition across the mountains into Spain and back.

The first day of the expedition woke us up to the reality of walking in big country. Through blistering heat we trudged uphill for five hours before lunch. Nobody went far without drinking heavily from their water-bottles.

Joanne found the journey difficult and was now beginning to struggle quite badly. Usually people found their legs after a couple of days, but poor Jo never really got into the stride. Each evening when people swam in the mountain lakes or chatted over cooking stoves, Joanne lay exhausted inside her tent. It was unusual for her; normally she kept herself fit and was quite a gritty character.

The expedition itself had many wonderful moments that stayed in my mind for a long time after. There were breathtaking views and incredible sunsets, as well as a wonderful peace and a sense of well-being beyond description.

After four days we'd toughened up considerably and became more than ready for a decent meal after suffering from the start with a mixture of dehydrated rations and tinned concoctions.

Day five saw three of us split off from the group to see what we could find at a mountain cafe we spotted on the map. Mercifully, after a long walk, we found it and entered like starving cowboys having crossed a desert. The little Brazilian lady ran to fetch us bowls of ice cream and cold drinks. After that, we tucked into the delights of French fries, omelette and hot coffee.

Such luxury made it incredibly hard to get up and resume the rigours of the course. We bought two big crates of beer, some wine and food, then set about carting it all down the valley for the others. The Brazilian lady was horrified that we should attempt carrying so much so far and offered to give us a ride in her car along a small road to the far end of the valley. It was with grateful relief we climbed into the car and set off along the twisting path, her legs so short that wooden blocks had been attached to the control pedals.

'Nice valley,' I commented, making small talk as we drove along.

As she looked at me to answer, the car drifted dangerously towards a big drop before she managed to snatch it back again. We were all gripping the seats in fear, but the lady drove on as if nothing had happened.

Without thinking, I instinctively spoke to her again a few minutes later. I regretted it as soon as the words crossed my lips. Once more she looked across to answer while the car skimmed the edge of the road.

'Shut it, Jimmy!' hissed the lads in the back through clenched teeth, their eyes piercing the back of my head in bewildered fear; they thought I was doing it for a laugh!

The lady continued driving along, smiling, oblivious to the near heart seizures taking place all around, until we reached the head of the valley. The lads scrambled out quickly to unpack the goods while I stayed to chat with the lady for a few moments. Remembering it was Joanne's birthday in a couple of days I arranged with her to supply a cake with candles. We'd return to her cafe after the expedition for a surprise party.

Meanwhile, the group, feeling in a celebratory mood after having almost completed the expedition, lit a big fire and sat around drinking, eating, singing, dancing and generally having a good time. We were up until the early hours. Then, one by one, everybody drifted off to sleep soundly in their sleeping-bags.

In the morning, as the sun rose above the surrounding crags, I woke to the comical picture of empty bottles stuffed into crates, a fire smouldering lightly and everybody scattered around me dozing.

It was with relative ease that we completed the final day and slumped triumphantly into our tents at base camp. That evening, after a good wash and change of clothes, we set off for a walk to the cafe. It was lovely strolling along in comfortable trainers without the dreaded rucksack for company. We looked a healthy bunch, our bronzed skin glowing against the bright colours of cotton clothing.

At the cafe we feasted to our hearts' content around a big table, each toasting the others' success in completing the expedition. A number of French people arrived to fill the place. We shared plenty of laughter with them. The Brazilian lady dug out some old Beatles music for us all to sing to—it was the most rowdy night the place had ever seen.

Halfway through the proceedings, I sneaked into the kitchen to light the candles on the cake. Then we dimmed the lights and brought it in ablaze.

Joanne cheered with everybody else, wondering whose birthday it was, until the cake came her way and everybody turned to cheer her. The surprise brought tears to her eyes as we roared out a chorus of *Happy Birthday*.

Joanne's bewilderment was further increased when I produced the gold chain and fastened it round her neck. Everybody insisted we dance together and cheered as we moved slowly across the floor. We began to kiss but broke off, laughing, as wolf whistles filled the air. It was a great night that neither of us will ever forget.

The following morning we all decided to set off early in order to spend a day in Paris on the way home. It was another long drive, during which Joanne's health played up again—she felt sick for most of the way. After camping at a seedy site on the edge of the city, we took to the streets for a long walk through the major sights. The wide, pedestrianised avenues were filled with tourists from all over the world, beating paths through mile after mile of traders and pavement artists, all vying for cash.

My mind was cast back almost two years to my previous failings on these familiar streets. Genevieve's parting swipe: 'Go back to your God,' rang afresh in my ears, the memory sending a shiver down my spine. Now, with Joanne at my side, the old and the new were brought together, curdling uncomfortably in my mind.

There was Denny, too, that crooked, scornful smile breaking out across a cheeky face that masked a struggle between madness and sadness. We'd almost lost touch, but I still wanted to see him again.

In the afternoon, Joanne and I set off to look around Denny's old haunts in an effort to find him. But in a city so big, busy, frantic and ever-changing, our effort was like a drop in the ocean. After an hour we gave up, rejoining the group on the tourist trail before finding the minibus in the evening.

The journey home was long and hard, Kenny alternating the

driving with me in a nonstop shuttle. The group tried to sleep, slouching uncomfortably against one another. Coming home was always difficult; throughout the years I spent working on Fairbridge Drake courses it never became any easier. Spending time in beautiful areas like the Pyrenees, Scotland, North Wales, the Lake District or the Yorkshire Dales made city life seem more ugly than ever.

Within a week of arriving home we discovered Joanne was pregnant. That explained why she'd found the Pyrenees trip so difficult. We were excited by the news and began buying all sorts of reading material on the subject.

Joanne persevered at college for as long as she could, but after seven months of pregnancy she had to stop. It signalled the end of her degree, which was an indication of our immaturity in terms of planning for the future.

Problems continued at the mission, and things grew particularly bad at Sunday school. Older lads were beginning to turn up to reign terror on the kids and threaten the helpers. It was as if something *possessed* them to hate us and the building so much.

Because Joanne was pregnant, I grew increasingly concerned about her involvement at the mission on the Sundays I worked away. Things came to a head when a gang trapped her in the entranceway. They had the little ones crying with fear, and they swore abuse at Joanne.

After talking with the pastor, we decided to call a halt to the Sunday school. It took all my will power to refrain from sorting out one particular young man who was the protagonist among the gang. I knew he was a big-mouthed coward who'd crumble if challenged alone, but confronting him would only serve to stir up more trouble, so I left it.

Life was becoming difficult for me. Besides working with many tearaways day after day, I came home to more of them ripping up the street, then suffered their intimidation each Sunday at church. I felt like a sitting duck just waiting for the next incident, my stomach churning with anxiety day after day.

Joanne, who'd already learnt how to trust God in a personal way after the burglary, was able to operate with a lot more peace than me. Many nights I slumped moodily into a chair, complaining about everything under the sun, even hating my own life. In my innermost being I knew I was having a lot of trouble trusting God really to look after me.

For a long time we held a Bible study in our house on Tuesday nights, which attracted an odd assortment of misfits. Those who came along seemed to be drawn from the scrap-heap of life, and they enjoyed the company each week. The studies were a good forum to hear wide-ranging points of view. When the study was over, we'd get stuck into stacks of toast and mugs of tea.

Our house served as an attraction for all sorts of people during the five years we were there. One visitor, a homosexual young man who used drugs, came knocking one night. I knew him from work, where he'd completed a course. He regularly called in for a chat. Like many others he'd succumbed to the temptation of the fruit offered on the street and had become addicted to a lifestyle that would destroy him.

He sat with us, looking uncomfortable, describing how his life had become a mess and how lost he felt. After listening for a while I heard myself ask, 'What are you looking for, Paul?'

'I don't know.'

'Do you want Jesus to rescue you like he rescued me?'

'Yeah, I do,' he answered, looking me squarely in the eye.

As we knelt down together and he began to pray, floods of tears broke out until he wept uncontrollably before God. It was incredible watching him go through this experience. He had all sorts of visions springing up in his mind.

Later, when things had calmed down, I showed him some verses in the Bible that would help him understand what had happened. He sat in a big armchair clutching that Bible for two days saying, 'God's in this house—I'm staying.'

We lived around him until he felt able to leave, but not until we'd convinced him that God would now be with him no matter where he went.

The day after Paul left, a young married mother from our street called round. She seemed on edge as we chatted. Then, with the same feeling I'd felt about Paul, I said, 'Julie, do you want to ask Jesus to come into your life right now?'

'Oh, yes, I do!' she blurted out. Then, with her head in her hands, she wept great sobs while crying out to God. She, like Paul, passed through an amazing experience into a new life in Christ. But in both cases they'd had to come to the end of themselves.

Joanne and I wondered what might happen next as these incidents had caught us completely by surprise. Two days later we got a visit from Michael, a strange young man who attended the Bible studies and spent his days walking the streets. All previous conversation I'd tried to spark up with him had been like flogging a dead horse. He was deep and very unhappy.

This night, though, he seemed a little more talkative. Among other things, he asked me about what it meant to be a Christian. Before long, the urge came over me to ask him the same question I'd asked the others: 'Michael, do you want to give your life to Jesus tonight? He loves you and he's just waiting to be asked.'

'Yes,' he answered quite definitely.

We knelt down to pray, but as hard as he tried he seemed to be wrestling with something inside that continually made him angry. In an effort to help, I prayed for him. As I did, something seemed to lift off his back and pass across mine. The whole room grew cold. This thing felt like a soggy wet blanket. It was horrible.

Although I'd heard about spiritual darkness, I'd never come across anything overtly evil—not until then. Michael left the house feeling as pent-up in his spiritual prison as when he'd arrived.

It had been an interesting week, two people unexpectedly becoming Christians and another seemingly unable to break out of his spiritual entanglements.

Back at work our new team leader arrived. Nick Gannicliffe was a man under whom I would grow considerably over the next 18 months. Unlike many other leaders who hog their position, Nick allowed me into the decision-making process more and more. This drew out my strengths as a leader but also highlighted weaknesses where training was needed. It was a refreshing partnership that helped me view my position in a more professional light.

Fairbridge Drake as a national charity with teams in many big cities was becoming more thorough in its procedures as each year passed by. If I was to gain future promotion I'd have to demonstrate the full range of skills needed.

When I arrived home from work one evening, Joanne told me she'd been having regular contractions all afternoon. Although Joanne had been pregnant for nine months, it suddenly dawned on me that I was about to become a father!

We settled down for the evening, keeping track of the intervals between contractions. Later, we decided to go to the hospital. We went feeling very excited. It was a long night, watching the monitor, me helping Joanne breathe easily and comforting her.

The process went on and on into the early hours. Eventually, the doctors came in to deliver the baby but, for some unknown reason, the baby wouldn't come out, and the doctors became increasingly concerned for the baby's well-being. Joanne had been through so many contractions that she was delirious under the injections given her.

Finally they had to use forceps. I'd never seen anybody suffer so much pain in all my life; it was terrible. After what seemed an eternity a little girl was produced. I almost collapsed with all the stress and exhaustion.

We called our lovely little daughter Sarah Jane. She weighed 8lb 9oz and was in perfect health.

Joanne's mother, who'd driven over from Nottingham, waited anxiously in the corridor for news of the outcome. When I stepped outside to tell her, I burst into tears on her shoulder. It had all been too much.

Joanne needed a whole week in hospital before being allowed home. When she was released, I took two weeks off work to look after both of them.

It was incredible how—much as we loved her—this tiny person came along and literally dominated our lives completely. We listened out for her every noise, took care of all possible comforts and cared until it ached. The presents, cards, visits, phone calls and well-wishes from work, church, family and friends came like a flood. We didn't realise we knew so many people.

But just a few days before my return to work, Joanne began haemorrhaging badly, blood pouring everywhere. An ambulance was called to rush her into hospital. Poor Joanne had already been through so much—and now this. I was left holding little Sarah in the hospital room while they wheeled Joanne away for an emergency operation.

In confusion, I didn't know whether she'd live or die. The stress of the past few weeks had been hard enough to bear; waiting in that half-lit room made things worse by the minute.

After what seemed an age, a nurse appeared, smiling. The operation had been a success and Joanne was fine. Having a baby enter our lives was a crisis in itself, but with these added complications to contend with, our memory of childbirth wasn't a healthy one.

Joanne took some time to regain her strength. Little Sarah, on the other hand, was bursting with newness of life and brought us a lot of joy. Because of Joanne's delicate condition, my protective instincts for both her and the baby convinced me that we needed to change churches. There was another church nearby called Emmanuel that had several young families like ourselves. We knew a number of people there and I was already acquainted with the pastor, Roger.

Leaving the mission was emotionally difficult; it had been my first church and I'd begun to grow under their loving care. The small congregation were very encouraging to us, wishing us well in our new place of worship.

On the eve of our leaving, an incident flared up that sent shockwaves right through my system.

While I was sitting in our living room talking to Joanne, the baby on my knee, a thunderous crash nearly caved our front door in. As I passed the now crying baby to Joanne another crash hit the door. My mind went blank as I stormed down the hall towards the front door. It was like a flashback to the violent days of my past.

I opened it to see Michael leap forward, screaming at me. Instinctively, my fist hit him square in the face, knocking him backwards. After quickly throwing him to the ground and grabbing him tightly around the throat, I ordered him out of the street. Then, before the neighbours had a chance to shift back their net curtains for a look, I was up, walking back to our door, where Joanne now stood holding Sarah.

Suddenly, she screamed, *'Jimmy, watch out!'*

I turned to see Michael flying at me again. Instinctively, I suspected he had a weapon, so I knocked him semiconscious on to the pavement with a volley of punches. The neighbours were all at the windows as I dragged him back to his feet and sent him staggering down the road. They must have been wondering what kind of Christianity I was into—maybe a John Wayne variety from the USA!

I walked back into the house feeling the sickness of adrenaline. It was hard to believe what had taken place. I was a Christian who should set an example. Not only was I supposed to avoid violence; I somehow thought being a Christian meant nothing like this could ever happen. It was very confusing.

For two years I'd tried hard to help Michael, only for it to end with me flattening him. What a failure I felt! Then it occurred to me that he may go to the police to press charges. Courtrooms, prisons, cells and my bad record ran through my mind. I quickly raced three doors down to Mr and Mrs Bow's house, an old couple.

'Mr Bow, can I use your phone to ring the police?'

'Yes, James, come in. What's the matter?' he asked in his gritty voice.

After explaining the incident and telling him I wanted to set the record straight with the police, he agreed warmly. Mrs Bow sat looking shocked.

'Mrs Bow and I saw it, James. Terrible, terrible,' he said. 'Nobody's safe any more. We're sick of it around here. It used to be a nice street, but not any more, not with nutters like him running around. And the profanities out of him, James! I had to cover Mrs Bow's ears. We know it wasn't you, James. It was that other fella.'

Mr Bow seemed to have a high regard for me, so I didn't have the heart to admit the bad language had come from *me!*

After talking to the police, I thanked Mr Bow and turned to leave. On the doorstep he stopped me to say, 'You're having it tough, son, what with the burglary, then the wife having a difficult birth and now this. But you'll make it, lad—we all had to after the war.'

In that moment I began to understand a little about how other people had fought their way through life. I could imagine the struggles he'd been through.

After a short wait the police arrived and my nerves calmed down.

'Don't worry, Mr Rice. We're getting calls like this all the time. We'll make sure a squad car patrols your house regularly for a few days and if you see the man nearby again, please ring us straightaway.'

It was a relief to know there'd be no prosecution from the police, though the incident itself left me feeling stunned.

That night Joanne and I laughed together about Mr Bow covering Mrs Bow's ears against the profanities. It still seems funny today.

Things seemed almost back to normal. But deep inside me I knew that I still hadn't effectively dealt a death blow to my tendency to violence.

10
Growing pains

Having joined a new church, I decided it was important to level with the pastor about the punch-up in the street. His calm reaction and loving support lifted me back on my feet and made it easy for me to be honest with him about any future problems I might have.

An important lesson Joanne and I learnt from our experience with Michael concerned time-wasters. Anyone who shows care and a willingness to help will inevitably attract problem people. Among them will be those who don't really *want* answers. Given the chance, they'll suck on you like a leech until you're empty and worn out.

As we've helped many people over the years, we've had to show tough honesty in equal measure to compassion. For example, while camped in the Lake District with a group some years ago, I decided to walk up a small hill in the evening to watch the sun go down. A young man with huge problems asked whether he could join me, so we walked together.

During our stroll he asked several questions. This led me to reveal that I'd once been a violent criminal. Such was his surprise that he pressed me further to find out what had changed me.

'I cried out to God for help, and Jesus came into my life. I've never been the same since.'

After walking along quietly for a while, he suddenly fell to his knees in the dust and began crying out to God to rescue his life. That young man was converted right in the middle of a dirt path at sunset.

Back in Birkenhead we unpacked the kit, issued certificates, then allowed everybody to go home. Later in the afternoon the same young man returned, carrying all his belongings, to say his girlfriend had kicked him out and he had nowhere to go. This immediately put me under pressure. But, after giving him a cup of tea, I rang a friend, who said he might be able to find him a place in the hostel where he worked.

'What am I going to do?' the young man kept asking me, meaning: 'What are *you* going to do?'

When we arrived at the hostel, it wasn't initially clear whether he'd be given a room or not. While we waited in the foyer, he said to me, 'Why can't I come and stay at *your* house?'

Once again I felt under pressure. But after a pause I pulled him to one side and said, 'Listen, buster. I'm helping you as much as I can, but I know what you're trying to do. You want to push me so hard I'll let you down, then you'll blame me and feel sorry for yourself. Well, don't go laying things on me, because it won't work. I'll help you stand on your own two feet if that's what you really want. So, what's it to be?'

He looked at me in wide-eyed amazement, then coyly admitted I was right. After that, he perked up again. We got him a room in the hostel and from there we began helping him get his life back together. I had to be tough with him in order to wake him up. Only *then* could he begin the task of sorting out his life.

Things at work seemed settled, and joining Emmanuel Church had proved a good move, but I continued to be plagued by all sorts of fears.

Vandalism, burglaries, fights, general disturbances and almost open heroin dealing went on all around in the streets. In the past I'd have simply removed myself from a situation that brought discomfort or held a threat, but I was tied to the streets. Running away would mean avoiding lessons I'd have to be brought back to learn another time.

I knew God was engineering my circumstances to teach me things, but trusting him was easier said than done. My sulky moods developed into pits of depression that often lasted days. I deflected the blame for my problems on our house, the street and even Joanne herself. This affected our relationship in every way. Then we found ourselves arguing regularly. My success and popularity at work only highlighted the misery of home life.

On one particular night I ranted up and down about everything, throwing accusations at Joanne as she sat on the end of the bed, feeling completely exasperated. We wanted so much to have a good relationship, to be friends as we'd been previously and to trust one another. But on this particular occasion we calmly agreed that no matter how hard we tried, it just wasn't working out. Sarah lay sleeping in her cot in the next room, which made things even worse.

'Let's just say a little prayer,' I suggested.

'OK,' Joanne said wearily.

'Oh, God, we don't know what to do. We've come to the end of ourselves. Can you help? Amen.'

I then went downstairs to make a cup of tea, intent on sleeping on the couch. Though I'd prayed that prayer, I didn't really expect an answer. Our marriage was through.

As the kettle boiled, the phone rang. It was nearly midnight. 'Who could that be at this hour?' I thought.

'Hello,' I answered.

'Jimmy? Jimmy, Jimmy, Jimmy!' drawled the American voice of my old friend David Fox from Ohio.

'I was just thinking about you there. Hey, don't ever let me hear you talk about divorce, you hear me? I've been counselling a man who's just been through his second divorce and boy, oh, boy, Jimmy, the *pain* that man's going through!'

I couldn't believe what I was hearing. Surely it was a coincidence? How could he have known what to say?

'Jimmy! How are you?' he eventually asked.

'All the better for hearing you,' I said, still feeling stunned by his message. We chatted for a minute or so before hanging up, then I made Joanne a cup of tea along with my own and took it upstairs.

'Oh, thanks,' she said, looking surprised.

'Guess who that was on the phone?'

'Who?'

'David Fox,' I said. 'Do you know what he said . . . .'

As I shared his message we both began to smile and then to laugh. We embraced once more and cried together. Despite our problems, we loved each other very much and desperately wanted our marriage to work out.

Before going to sleep we prayed another short prayer, this time a prayer of thanks to God for helping us over this latest obstacle.

During those early years of marriage, we stumbled through many such difficult times, never quite giving up hope of working it out together. I was often reminded of the vision God gave me before we committed ourselves to marriage—all the reality of the odds and ends represented on that old table-top was coming true.

Our new church had a membership scheme, a condition of which was abstinence from alcohol. Although we were growing in the understanding of our faith week by week, I occasionally drank too much and made a fool of myself.

In an effort to put an end to this occasional but destructive habit, we decided to become church members. I thought making a promise to such an established church was sure to keep me off the bottle. But the underlying problems that caused my anxieties, depression and need for the occasional booze-up remained unresolved.

Eighteen months after Nick's arrival as team leader at work, he decided to resign and further his career with another organisation in the Lake District. It was a sad loss. I'd flourished well under his leadership, becoming proficient in all aspects of the work.

His departure signalled the arrival of a replacement, but despite my having most of the qualities needed to do the job myself, my formal qualifications were incomplete.

I watched with interest the kind of people who began applying for the job and found to my interest that none of them were any more capable than me. In fear of coming under the leadership of somebody less proficient, I decided to apply for the job myself. Joanne and I grew quite excited about the prospect of my promotion. It would mean more money and add substance to my employment credentials.

Two major questions on the application form asked what personal qualities I'd bring to the position and what plans I had for the further development of our work with young people. At first glance they seemed tricky questions. But when I thought about them, my mind was bursting with ideas just waiting to get out.

Added to this was my genuine concern for the youngsters we worked with. I wanted to help them as much as I'd been helped myself. I simply poured out my ideas and feelings on to paper, then mailed the application form off to our directors in London.

When I received a letter inviting me to an interview, I suddenly realised I'd never had a proper one in my life. On the train journey to London I felt nervous, imagining the many questions they might ask. It made me realise how difficult interviews could be.

At our central office the two directors, who I knew quite well, welcomed me and got proceedings off to a quick start. Amazingly, they both thought my rehabilitation from crime was the sole result of taking part in a couple of their courses. In seeking to put them in the picture we spent almost two hours talking about my Christian faith!

To my surprise, the interview was very enjoyable and this helped us get to know each other much better. Eventually, they asked me to wait outside their office for a while until they'd come to a decision.

Sitting there alone waiting for an answer was uncomfortable to say the least; I couldn't bear the thought of their refusing me. The waiting, however, didn't last long. They soon called me back inside, shook my hand and congratulated me on gaining the position.

I was absolutely thrilled. Then I had the same feeling I'd experienced when I was originally given the instructor's job: the desperate need to get outside and breathe some fresh air.

As soon as the pleasantries were over, I excused myself from the office and set off walking briskly around London's West End. What a relief to get the job! This was a big step forward in my march away from the past. I'd been out of prison four years and things were going well.

Joanne was excited when I rang to pass on the good news—it was just the kind of encouragement we needed.

Before walking to the station for the journey home, I called into a burger bar on Oxford Street for a bite to eat. Sitting there eating brought back memories of old. Many times I'd walked along this street without money, feeling lonely and hungry. I'd envied those who seemed able to buy any food they wanted and sit eating with friends.

As I looked out at the passers-by on this grey day I wondered whether somebody may be looking at me with the same green envy. Nothing ever seemed to change. Jesus once said, 'The poor you will always have with you.'

After writing so many wonderfully supportive letters and becoming a real pillar in my life, David Fox now wrote to say he'd be coming over from the USA for a short visit. Joanne would finally get to meet this great old friend of mine.

When he arrived, David spent a few days with us in Paterson Street before I took him to Scotland sightseeing for five days. David loved me as a son and was excited to see me growing in my faith. Besides treating me with care, he pushed me hard to attain greater understanding.

Old men who can trace wasted opportunities in their younger years often pin great hope on today's young men. They want to see them setting their faces like flint to serve the living God and ignoring the petty attractions all around that so easily ensnare. David could see lots of potential in me to become a great weapon in God's hand. But there were many facets of my personality that needed adjustment.

'I've come to bug you,' David said in his broad Ohio accent as we headed north up the motorway. 'I've come to razz you, Jimmy.'

And boy, did he razz me, prodding away each day, trying to unhinge the mask behind which he knew my insecurities lay!

We stayed at my friend Des Dugan's house up in the Cairngorms of Scotland for the first couple of days. It's a very dramatic area that David enjoyed enormously. After that, we headed down the west coast through the beautiful glens, towering hillsides, crystal-clear lochs and green countryside towards Oban.

We booked into a hotel and spent a couple of days sightseeing around the many local islands and bays. David continued to challenge something in me that he knew wasn't right.

One night as we sat in the hotel room, I guess he said something that struck a chord. Some hidden door inside me seemed to open up. It felt as if my whole insides were a fiery chasm.

'Are you all right?' David asked.

'Just be quiet or I'll wreck the whole hotel.'

He sat across the room looking worried as I tried to regain control. It was my first look at the tempest that still raged within. After a while I decided to go out for a walk on my own, but David insisted on coming along. The wind blew hard as I strode along, making it difficult for him to keep up. My anger was rising at not being given enough space.

His breathing grew more difficult as we slowly climbed the steep paths leading to McCaig's Tower high above the town.

'Why do you bother with me?' I shouted at him.

'Well, Jimmy,' he said leaning against a stone wall to catch his breath, 'you're an unusual young man.'

'But what's that mean? I'm no different from anybody else. What is it that keeps you chasing me, writing to me, forgiving me, caring for me? You've never told me why.'

I stood staring at him.

'Oh, Jimmy, Jimmy,' he said, shaking his head, still leaning against the wall.

I walked on, feeling frustrated that he wouldn't answer my question properly. He tagged on behind again, breathing with difficulty as before.

'You don't even know why yourself, do you? You're trying to think up a smart answer for me.'

I stared at him in annoyance, but he didn't respond.

After walking on, I stopped again to say, 'You're just getting old. You're trying to keep up with me in some way to be young again. You're making a fool of yourself.'

I walked on again, reaching the neon-lit balcony at the tower where my love for Joanne had been ignited all those years before. After a minute he caught me up again and stood panting at my side. My words didn't seem to have had any effect on his care for me.

'What is it, David? What's it all about?'

'Young man, when we prayed in your room that day when we first met, I saw the Holy Spirit come down on you in such a way. Boy, oh, boy . . . .'

He trailed off without completing his sentence.

'I still don't know what you're talking about. Why can't you make yourself plain?' I felt exasperated.

'You wanna know what I saw, do you? Well, I'll tell you. After I'm dead the Lord Jesus will return. That's what I saw. And before that you'll raise the dead, heal the sick and help the blind see.'

He looked away in silence as if he'd said something he shouldn't have. I felt embarrassed at having pushed him so far. It was as if he'd been forced by one of his own children to hand out Christmas presents early, only to regret it. I could barely take in what he'd said.

We stood in silence looking out over the harbour, the wind blowing fiercely through our hair.

'Come on,' he said, putting his hand on my shoulder. We walked back to the hotel quietly. We'd reached a point where we'd broken each other; he seemed humiliated.

The following day we completed the long drive back to my house, where we only had time to sleep before getting up for the final leg to Heathrow Airport.

When he'd gone I hardly knew what to make of his visit. We seemed to have been at odds for most of the time.

David's first letters after his arrival home suggested he, too, was struggling to make sense of the visit. His constant wish was to be a source of encouragement to me. Although he'd been on the right track in bugging me, he feared he'd sent our friendship tumbling backwards. For any relationship to become secure it has to be proved through the stormy tempests.

Meanwhile at work, things were going from strength to strength. After initially feeling a little isolated following Nick's departure, I soon got my teeth into the job.

Being slightly underqualified served to make me work all the harder, striving to produce the best possible courses. We visited new areas in which to operate, trying all sorts of different activities that proved effective. That summer of 1987 working alongside Mick Greenwood as my main instructor was the most enjoyable working experience of my life.

At church, too, Joanne and I continued to develop. We made new friends and joined the adult Sunday school, where I became a group leader. We looked on ourselves as children in a Christian sense, taking a lead from the more mature people around us who seemed further on in their faith.

But despite these encouraging signs, things at home were still difficult. David Fox, with his bullish approach, seemed to have dislodged things that now bubbled up to the surface. My reactions to the increased disturbances in the street were rooted in fear, making me over-react every time.

Fear of criticism made it impossible for Joanne to win an argument. I blasted her, the street and the church with stinging comments, only to fall into terrible regret afterwards. One particular night I moaned about everything until the early hours. Whenever it seemed as if I was about to calm down, another torrent of garbage came spewing out of my mouth.

Joanne was numb with tiredness, completely sick of my impossible ways and sat slumped in dejection.

Finally, during the early hours of the morning, I fell to my knees in tears, weeping before God for help.

'I've had enough, God. I can't take any more—this area's too tough for me. You've got to let me out of the situation before I crack up. I can't do it; I'm not strong enough. I'm weak, I'm nothing. I admit it, so let's just call it a day.'

As I knelt there sobbing, I knew God was opening the door for me to go. Relief filled me like warm light.

'That's it, Jo,' I said. 'He's letting me out of the situation. We'll move house and things'll be all right.'

We sat in silence for a few moments before I spoke again.

'Hang on a minute. Let me just pray another prayer,' I said. 'Dear God, thanks for letting me out of this situation, but can I put a condition on it? If I've got to come back at a later date in order to learn whatever lesson you're trying to teach me, then I'd prefer to stay and see it through.'

Joanne could hardly believe I could say such a thing after all the pain of the night. I'd taken another difficult step on my journey, but somewhere along the line we needed to make a real breakthrough, otherwise our marriage would simply fall apart.

During this time, an old man who often attended my Bible study group died. His name was Maynard James. He'd been a street evangelist for a great many years and had the warm respect of everybody who knew him. His humble graciousness drew me to him, and I was sad to see him go.

Having missed his funeral because of working away, I attended his memorial service, which took place in Yorkshire. The hall was filled with high-ranking ministers, college principals and assorted guests from far and wide. It was fascinating to hear the various accounts of Maynard's life spoken by the string of people who visited the pulpit.

One consistent theme that struck me was that Maynard was never heard to criticise another man. What a great thing to be remembered for in today's cut-throat world!

The main speaker was a South African who was the principal of a Bible college in Edinburgh.

'You've heard much about the life of our dear departed brother, Maynard James,' he began. 'I'd like to concentrate on the message he constantly preached up and down this land, a message that transformed many lives.'

The principal's preaching was powerful and clear, taking us through the many problems Christians are plagued with, then on to outline the solutions Jesus brings us in the Bible. There came a point where his words had me completely rooted, reminding me graphically of the mess my home life was in. He went on to say that Christ could enter into our hearts in fulness, flushing out the dregs of badness inside.

'That's what I want,' I suddenly said, half standing to interrupt. *'I want Jesus in my heart just like you said.'*

All eyes turned to me, but I hardly noticed, such was the intensity of my effort to capture the moment.

'Well—er—if you'll allow me to finish, maybe we can have an appeal at the end.'

I sat down again as he resumed his sermon, waiting anxiously for the conclusion in order to respond. At the end he invited people to come forward for prayer during the closing hymn. Along with a number of others, I went forward and knelt quietly at the rail as they sang.

After a few moments Roger, my pastor, knelt with me. As his hand rested on my shoulder to offer comfort, something broke within. All the hurt, frustration, fear and disappointment of recent years poured out. In sobbing tears I kept repeating to God: 'I just want to be a good husband and dad, that's all I want—to be good for them.'

We remained at the rail for what seemed an eternity. In my mind I hoped that God had cured me from being a fool.

My response at that meeting was one of many efforts made in search of a miracle solution to my personality. I thought God would wave a magic wand and turn me into Mr Niceguy, if I looked hard enough. But despite his divine intervention at key points along the way, the main tactic was a long siege in which he continually drew my dross to the surface.

I returned home feeling encouraged but knowing tough times still lay ahead. Joanne hung on to every one of these little breakthroughs in the desperate hope that one day we'd establish a more peaceful relationship.

Little did she realise the trauma I'd have to go through before that could be achieved.

11
Fighting for life

In the same way that I'd been asked to gain a driving licence to fulfil my obligations as an instructor, I was now asked to gain a mountain leadership certificate to meet the requirements of a team leader.

It was a difficult qualification to gain, beginning with at least two years' experience documented in a log book, then five days' intensive training at an authorised centre, covering all aspects of the craft. A year then had to elapse before embarking on the assessment, which included six full days of being tested in everything.

I had over three years' solid experience in leading groups, and I'd completed my training. Now I was all set for the dreaded assessment. I arranged to visit North Wales with a friend for a few days to sharpen up my skills before tackling the rigorous test.

The day before we were due to depart, I felt some kind of bug coming on which set my shoulders tingling and head aching. We postponed the trip a day so I could get some antibiotics from the doctor. I wasn't used to illness holding me back from anything; I usually just ignored it and carried on.

The doctor couldn't find anything wrong. He told me to take some mild painkillers and let him know what happened. That night I was kept wide awake by a throbbing headache mixed with severe feelings of flu. The doctor visited me the following day but still couldn't find exactly what was wrong. He told me to continue with the painkillers and keep him informed.

On that second night, besides my throbbing head, I began to vomit violently. Two nights without sleep left me feeling a wreck. When the doctor heard how I was, he rang for an ambulance to take me immediately to hospital.

Despite feeling pretty rotten, I couldn't understand what the fuss was all about. Why an ambulance? When it arrived, the two men brought a special chair to carry me out of the house.

'What's all this about?' I thought, putting on a brave face and getting ready to walk out by myself. But to my surprise, I couldn't stand, let alone walk.

During the ride to hospital and subsequent transfer to an isolation room I felt even worse. The nurses had to keep the room darkened because the light sent terrible pain into my head. Doctors came to carry out various tests in an effort to find out what my problem was.

That night I became delirious with pain. I was rolling round the bed having terrible nightmares. One minute I was shaking uncontrollably with cold, the next almost suffocating with heat.

My family visited, but as the days went by I had no idea what I was talking about or what was going on. The doctors struggled to find out the cause of my illness, but for now it remained a mystery.

I vomited everything that passed my lips, had needles poked in me day and night, couldn't urinate and was becoming thinner by the minute.

The main clue to the problem came after a few days, when my calf muscles seized up, causing me excruciating leg pain. Apparently, this symptom is linked to a disease called leptospirosis, or Weil's disease.

Just five days after arriving in hospital my kidneys failed and the walls of my stomach began to collapse, causing me to vomit blood all over the bed. I was taken into intensive care, where all kinds of needles and tubes were attached to various parts of my body.

With my skin completely yellow, and my bones protruding because of weight loss, I looked almost dead. Joanne, my family, my pastor and all those who knew me were in dazed shock as, after only a week in hospital, I now faced death. The doctors, feeling 80 per cent sure about the cause of my illness, had begun to administer the appropriate antibiotic. My whole church, along with many others who knew me, were on their knees praying to God day and night.

During this critical time when the antibiotics had to do battle with the bacteria, nobody knew what the outcome might be. Then, early one morning on a visit, Joanne noticed urine in my bag, an indication that my kidneys had begun to function once again. The doctors confirmed that I'd started to stabilise and, while I continued to be very ill, things weren't getting any worse.

Joanne knew deep within that I'd turned the corner and was on the road to recovery. Sure enough, I slowly began to move away from death's door. After a few days they put me back into an ordinary room. Such had been my delirium that I thought I'd only spent an afternoon instead of several days in intensive care!

Each day, the nurses injected the antibiotic to kill off all trace of the disease; my veins ached with the continual bombardment. The doctors told me that leptospirosis was caused by a bacterium that germinated in rat's urine. If a person came into contact with a patch of water infected with it, the disease could get in through eyes, nose, mouth, ears, fingernails or cuts.

It was obvious I'd caught it while out canoeing with the groups at work, but from which stretch of water I didn't know. My own guess was that it came from a canal in Chester, where I could remember swallowing dirty water after falling in while messing around.

During the next week I was visited by a continual stream of people who brought cards, gifts, food and well wishes. The fact that I couldn't go home, do any work or even look after myself properly released me into an experience of rest I'd never known before.

Lying on my bed looking out at the Wirral countryside brought me complete peace; no worry entered my mind. Each morning I watched the sun rise slowly, dispersing the mist from around the legs of the woodland as autumn colours appeared on the trees. I wanted to remain captured in this existence for as long as possible.

Back into my mind came the words of Nicky Cruz's dad, which I'd read in a book in prison years earlier. He described Nicky as a bird with no legs, always fluttering around, unable to come to a rest. That description suited *me*, too.

From this island of rest I could see that throughout my life my mind had never been restful. All my days I'd been running around, chasing, pushing and striving for something or other. Relaxation had seemed a waste of time.

This unexpected taste of luxurious peace has since led me to seek out and enjoy quiet moments whenever possible so I can forget the world's cares.

It wasn't long before the doctors allowed me home again. It was great to see little Sarah. She hadn't been allowed into the isolation ward where I'd been kept.

While still convalescing, I got news from Fairbridge Drake that one of the trustees, Major General Sir John Nelson, wanted to visit. I tried to put him off at first, thinking it a waste of time now I was recovering, but he insisted. So one afternoon as I lay on the couch, the rough kids in the street looked on in amazement as a chauffeur-driven Daimler cruised to a halt outside our door.

The chauffeur wisely stayed with the vehicle while Sir John came in. Joanne and I didn't know what to expect until a grey-haired, strapping old gentleman bounded into the room and flopped into a chair as if it were his own.

'Jimmy! Jim Rice, nice to meet you!' he said enthusiastically.

'Nice to meet you, too, Sir John. Please excuse me having to lie down.'

'Oh, not at all. You carry on,' he interjected. 'Now, Jimmy, I've heard a lot about you. You know the Lord, don't you?'

'I'm a Christian, if that's what you mean.'

'Great news. Well done!'

He went on to ask how I became a believer in Jesus Christ. Then, after a brief rendition, we talked nonstop for ages. We got on well, striking up a friendship that I've found supportive ever since. As a family we've visited and had holidays with him and his lovely wife, Lady Jane, at their home in Scotland.

Many times over the years, God has brought special people to operate alongside me, people like David Fox and Sir John Nelson, who have been a great encouragement.

After a couple of months' steady improvement I set a date for returning to work. In preparation, Joanne and I flew with Sarah to the Canary Islands for a sunny break. Having the sun on my back, swimming in the sea and generally running around served to lift my confidence for my return.

Shortly after arriving home, Joanne discovered she was pregnant again. We both wondered what it was about Spanish territory that brought these things on!

It was mid-February when I re-entered the office, looking overweight and brown as a berry. Everybody else seemed pale and ill-looking by comparison. Mine wasn't the sort of job where a back seat could be taken. My personality wouldn't allow it, anyway, so I got stuck in straightaway, running courses right through the summer.

Despite my appearing to do the job with my usual ease, as time went by I was finding it increasingly difficult. Sometimes while away camping with a group I wanted to throw in the towel and give up.

Joanne noticed the pressure building up into bouts of moodiness at home. She urged me to talk to somebody about it but, to her frustration, I couldn't bring myself to do so. Instead, like many men, I chose to drag my miserable frame around in the hope that it would all wear off.

Things came to a head one day when I blew my top in the house. After breaking some furniture in a rage, I punched a door off its hinges. Joanne and Sarah were crying in our bedroom upstairs while I shouted out of control. In the end I fell into a heap of tears, bitterly regretting what I'd done and crying out to God to help me.

Life was too difficult. I didn't know how to go on.

We phoned Roger, asking him to come around as quickly as possible, then sat waiting in silence. When he arrived we told him what had happened while he sat listening patiently.

Turning to me, he asked things like, 'What's been the matter? Why did you behave that way? Do you think Joanne deserves such treatment?'

During my long answer he broke in to say, *'Look at you!* You're full of self-pity. All you can think about is yourself. You're talking like a very selfish man.'

His words cut me to the heart. My anger rose sharply and for a minute I was on the verge of beating him up. But somehow I managed to sit tight, swallow his words, then look at him and say, 'You're right. I *am* full of self-pity and selfishness. I admit it.'

Having said it, I sat there feeling completely helpless. These horrible things had infested my personality like cancer. How could I *ever* get rid of them?

That admission was one of the most painful I'd ever had to make. For weeks afterwards the shame of them remained sharply in focus. Roger agreed to visit us each Tuesday night along with meeting us separately on a regular basis.

Joanne was completely at the end of her tether. She asked Roger in private, hopelessness written across her face, whether he thought I could ever change.

Roger had seen me break down in earnest at the memorial service, and had seen other signs along the way. He told Joanne he was convinced of my desire to change. It was only this assurance that kept Joanne going. She knew Roger spoke the truth; he'd have said the opposite about me had it been the case.

During a very sombre time of prayer the following day, Jesus came to me with the words: *'In commitment to me is all healing.'*

It was a simple statement that broke down all the complexities, floating through my troubled mind with a healing touch. It cast no judgment at all on my behaviour, but simply pointed in the direction of restoration.

My innermost being was suddenly filled with new hope. God was offering me access through a door that held the answers —commitment to Jesus! I refrained from making any grand promises to Joanne. She needed more than mere words. I simply told her the message and got on with it. In truth I'd never trusted God with our situation in the way Joanne had and, therefore, was never likely to find true peace.

After talking this through with Joanne we prayed together, making a fresh commitment to Christ. I also entrusted him with our lives in Birkenhead.

It's hard to describe the breakthrough this brought us, but suddenly we found ourselves able to cope. Nothing at all about our circumstances had changed, but somehow we were lifted above them into a new dimension. Trusting God wasn't so bad after all.

In meeting with Roger, I was able to confess quite openly to him—and to God in prayer—that I was guilty of self-pity and being selfish. After having embraced these negative habits as a young man, I'd become hopelessly bound up in them. Being a Christian meant God would continue setting me free from the hidden problems within.

A verse in the Bible (1 John 1:9) says: 'If we confess our sins, he is faithful and just and will forgive us our sins and purify us from all unrighteousness.'

Once again the God who'd rescued my imprisoned life was cutting me free from the things that held me down, things that men and women on their own find impossible to do anything about.

12
Breaking through

Another major development at that time came as a result of regular visits from our pastor, Roger. Although we'd explained to him the fluctuating tensions of living where we did, he never grasped their power until he'd walked the street and sat with us several times.

Quite often, as we began our meetings, Sarah woke up screaming. Kids arrived to smash things up in the back alley, the neighbour's dogs barked and arguments raged in nearby homes.

We'd never connected these events, but Roger did. He asked whether we knew of any dark spiritual activity taking place in the neighbourhood, such as ouija boards, witchcraft, Satanism or general occultism. We didn't know anybody specifically, but we knew those kind of things were practised in homes nearby.

Roger said that if any of those practices were going on in local homes, they'd noticeably affect the atmosphere of the street. We weren't sure what he was getting at. But he went on to say that a spiritual problem needed a spiritual answer, and he suggested that if we used Jesus' name to oppose these powers of darkness they'd have to submit.

We were immediately reminded of countless times in the Bible when Jesus opposed and defeated bad spirits whenever he encountered them. The Bible goes on to record how, after Jesus departed, he passed his Spirit on to believers like us so that we could perform the same task in his name.

What took place next was quite incredible. Roger, Joanne and I used Jesus' name in prayer to oppose the unseen powers of darkness in our streets. As we did this, peace suddenly descended on the whole place.

It was hard to believe we'd made any difference, and I wondered whether it was just a coincidence. We soon learnt it wasn't. Many times after that, whenever we felt an oppressive air fill the street, we opposed it in the name of Jesus and actually *felt* it disappear.

With a new-found willingness to trust God, a fresh commitment to Jesus and this awareness to fight a spiritual fight, my life took a leap forward.

At work, however, my physical health went from bad to worse. Because I felt continually weak, I tried to avoid as many tasks as possible. During the final summer course before my holiday, I had to rely on Mick to supervise the group through almost every activity while I struggled on in the background.

I was no longer able to do the job properly. If I persisted in carrying on, my health would become badly affected. In addition, Joanne was only a month away from giving birth to our second child. I began the summer break in a real dilemma. If I resigned, there wasn't any other work for me, yet my health wouldn't allow me to carry on.

Even though I'd professed faith in God, this test showed how unwilling I remained to trust him with my life. Each day I paced the floor, trying to understand the situation. But the more I looked, the less I could see.

During my daily Bible readings a message kept repeating itself in Jesus' words: 'My Father will give you whatever you ask in my name.'

That name of Jesus was coming up again: First, he was beating evil, now his name could unlock answers from God the Father. Such a wide-open promise left me wondering exactly what I *did* want (£1 million did cross my mind!).

With just a few days left before my return to work, I grabbed hold of this promise with both hands and began to pray:

'God, I've got to have an answer to my problem. You said I could have anything in Jesus' name, so I'm asking you in his name to give me a clear answer about work—before today's out.'

This, like many other conversations with God, was carried out while marching up and down, eyes wide open and hands waving around Italian-style to emphasise my point.

I decided not to eat all day in order to feel alert in case I missed the message. Most of the day passed without a whisper. Then in the evening I went back to prayer, thinking God hadn't heard or maybe had forgotten.

This time a clear message came into my mind. I was to listen to a tape David Fox had sent almost two years previously. After initially doubting whether God had *really* prompted me to listen to it, I put it on the tape deck to play. It was a sermon all about how God brings a man through a problem. Putting all other options to one side, David then turned his attention to the main theme of his message: 'Going back into the fire.'

Suddenly, I didn't like the sound of it.

As the tape reeled along, it became abundantly clear that the message for me was to go back into the fire, in other words, return to the job. Work had become so synonymous with pain, discomfort and frustration since my illness that the term 'fire' seemed an apt description.

Joanne came in and sat next to me while I listened.

'What's it like?' she asked.

'Stupid,' I answered.

As we sat together, I knew the message would become as clear to her as it was to me. There was no escaping it. When the tape finished I got to my feet and stomped up and down in annoyance.

'This is stupid,' I said. 'If I can't do the job, why do I have to go back? What's the point? Doesn't God know I'm sick and can't do the job properly? This is stupid, *stupid!*'

Joanne sat quietly while I got it out of my system but was surprised when I suddenly did a turnaround.

'. . . but OK, OK,' I continued. 'No matter how stupid it is, I'll go, I'll go. I promise. I'll do what you ask, then it's all up to you. It's not my fault if it all goes wrong.'

This attitude was the big breakthrough into faith that my life needed. I was prepared to trust God with a problem that didn't seem to have an answer. All too often I'd confined him to the limits of my own understanding. If I couldn't see a way through, there couldn't be one.

This time, I let go of the worry, washed my hands of the responsibility for finding a solution and rested firmly in faith.

David Fox had unwittingly reached across the Atlantic to 'razz' me once again.

Before returning to work, I visited my doctor to tell him about the sluggishness that was plaguing me there.

'You're fortunate to be alive, Mr Rice,' he replied. 'It'll take a couple of years before your body recovers from the illness. Take a month off. Then, when you've finished that, take another.'

His words left me confused about how things might develop. They appeared more complicated than ever. But true to my pledge I left the situation with God.

While I was off work, I wandered around aimlessly until I hit on the idea of visiting our church administrator, John Green, as he worked in the vestry. He and I decided to draw up a list of people who needed prayer, and we began petitioning God for them.

After we'd prayed through our list, John prayed about my situation but was interrupted by a phone call. He handed the receiver to me.

'It's for you, Jimmy.'

'It must be Joanne,' I thought.

'Jimmy, I'm terribly sorry to phone while you're at church,' said the distinct voice of Peter Lewis, my director in London.

'That's OK.' I felt totally amazed that he should ring me at all.

He went on to explain that, as a result of a considerable difference of opinion, my boss, Dougie, had resigned his job and left the office, never to return.

'Just want to keep you in the picture, Jim. You're the senior man at your end at the moment, so if anybody needs support, please oblige.'

'Yes, of course, Peter,' I replied before closing.

What an incredible turn of events! He and Dougie had locked horns on many occasions, but this must have been a bit special. It was all right asking me to support people, but what good was I now I was on the sick list?

I went home to tell Joanne the news. We were both sad. Dougie had always been very good to us over the years. We made lunch, then sat talking about it, when the phone rang. It was Peter Lewis again.

'Jimmy, have you ever considered stepping up to become the team manager yourself?'

His question caught me completely off balance.

'No, I haven't, Peter. I don't really want it.'

'Why's that, Jim?'

'Well, I feel confident in doing the job as it stands at the moment, but when all the new developments are added that've been mooted recently I wouldn't be able to cope.'

'Which developments do you mean?'

After I'd detailed them, he said, 'Jimmy, I hear what you're saying. But we've already decided not to press ahead with those particular developments anyway.'

'Oh,' I murmured in response.

'Will you come to London for a chat?'

All my reasons for refusing had been taken away. Now I felt inextricably drawn into this whole new situation. This time I'd be going to London not for a competitive interview but to be coaxed into a job. What a deal!

As with previous occasions, Joanne and I were absolutely thrilled. The manager's job brought better wages and much more time at home with the family. More important, after trusting God with a tricky situation, he'd come up with a perfect solution.

Before we had time to linger in the joy of that situation, it was time for Joanne to give birth to our second child. Quite conveniently, Joanne went into labour after Sarah had gone to sleep in the evening. This allowed the babysitter to arrive and release us to drive to the hospital without any fuss.

Within a few hours Joanne gave birth to our second daughter, Billie-Jean. It had been a straightforward delivery that went a long way to wiping out the painful memories of Sarah's troubled arrival. Like Sarah, Billie-Jean was in perfect health, weighing an ounce less than Sarah at 8lb 8oz.

With all the turmoil of recent weeks out of the way, I decided to sign off from sick leave and take up my new position at the office. It was quite a moment. Only four years previously I'd walked in off the street and been offered an instructor's job out of the blue. Now I was running the show.

As with the team leader's job, I began the team manager's job in slight trepidation. I missed the presence of my predecessor, wondering whether I could really hold the job down.

The days rolled into weeks and soon I got used to things. I began to enjoy it immensely. We'd been given notice of the expiry of our tenancy, so my first major task was to move the base from Birkenhead to Liverpool. Having operated out of the same building in Conway Street for over six years, the move was quite an upheaval for everyone.

As the move coincided with the year's end, we decided to throw a big Christmas party where we could celebrate the old and bring in the new. Dougie accepted our invitation to attend, which gave everybody the chance to say goodbye to him. The biggest cheer of the night went up when we presented him with a gift.

In the new year we moved across the river to a temporary base on Liverpool's dock-front while awaiting the conversion of a ship that would become our new floating centre. The ship took a year to complete, but when it was finished it looked a treat with its office atop and hall below. It also had kitchen, storerooms, staffroom, toilets and showers.

With some keen persuasion, we got permission from Merseyside Development Corporation to base ourselves within their prestigious docklands development, which included Albert Dock. It was a prime site, exposing us to the business community from which we needed sponsorship. It was also accessible by public transport for young people from all over Merseyside.

Besides running a relevant service to hard-bitten young people, we built up a very good team who genuinely cared about the work. We raised large amounts of funding, kept ourselves in the public eye, opened another office on the Wirral and began a lot of new work in Salford and Manchester.

Just like the instructor's and team leader's jobs, this one

stretched me to the limit, fulfilling all my potential over an exciting three-year period.

Shortly after starting the new job I had a visit from a social worker, Chris Ashley, about a young scallywag he was working with. As we talked, it became clear that Chris was a Christian who also did voluntary work with Prison Fellowship, an organisation that prays for and helps prisoners, ex-prisoners and their families.

With my background, he must have seen me as an ideal candidate for joining the Prison Fellowship support group he headed up. But despite the passage of years, anything to do with prisons made me feel uneasy. Seeing the Risley bus in the mornings was about my limit!

As time went by, however, I became more interested. The group sounded a nice bunch, so I went along. After going a few times, I became a regular attender.

Chris knew I'd served time in Stoke Heath Borstal a decade previously, so he asked me one day whether I'd go back in there one evening to speak to a group of lads. I agreed without really thinking about it. Whenever I was asked to speak to groups of young people, I usually just said yes and got on with it.

On the evening Chris was due to pick me up, old memories began to creep back into my mind along with feelings associated with my release from Stoke Heath all those years before. I wasn't used to sharing my fears with anybody, so I covered them up and carried on chatting as we drove along.

After a couple of hours, we drew near to the place. My stomach began screwing itself into a knot. I was distinctly uncomfortable. Old, forgotten faces popped back into my mind, along with the haunting memory of times spent in solitary confinement. For me, Stoke Heath spelt misery in every sense of the word.

We arrived a little early and sat in the car looking out at the gatehouse as we passed the time.

'What's it like seeing the place again, Jimmy?' Chris asked.

'Not bad,' I lied. 'It's just a bit weird, really.'

I remembered hating everybody in this place—screws and lads

alike. The only member of staff I ever spoke friendly to was Mr Jupp. It was hard to see why I liked him and not the others; maybe it was because he was a friendly guy. Then again, I'd hated plenty of friendly people, too!

While I sat there thinking, an officer appeared at the gate. As he stepped out to walk away, I recognised him immediately.

'That's Mr Jupp, isn't it, Chris?' I asked, opening the door to get out and say hello.

'Do you mean to say you know Roger Jupp?' asked Chris, looking surprised as we stepped out of the car. 'He became a Christian a few years ago.'

'Hi, Roger,' said Chris, getting his attention. 'Nice to see you again. How are you doing?'

After they'd shaken hands, Chris turned to me.

'Do you remember this fellow, Roger—about 10 years ago?'

Roger looked puzzled, his mind racing back and forth across the memory of countless faces he'd come across in the job over the years.

'Rice,' Chris suggested.

'Rice. Oh, yes, Ricey!' The memory came back in a flood.

We stood talking for a few minutes, laughing about old times and characters we could remember. Then it was time to go in.

Seeing Roger like that was a real blessing from God. It helped cushion the impact of my return, making it a little easier. Going back inside was a very strange experience. Everything seemed smaller than I'd remembered, yet by the look of it nothing had been altered.

The chapel was a new place for me; I'd never been in there while serving my sentence, not even at Christmas.

One of the lads who came to listen was well known to me. He lived near my house and had completed one of our courses at work. He was one of those characters for whom going to prison was an essential part of the image they wanted to construct.

Looking at him, along with many of the others, was like seeing a piece of my past. What could I say to help bring them back on to the right track? Many young people press the destruct button.

There's nothing anybody can do to stop them except keep the friendship going and pray that they'll show a desire to change before it's too late.

Mark Twain, the American writer, said: 'When I was 16 I realised I had a fool for a father. When I reached 21 I couldn't believe how much he had come on in the last five years.'

The only thing I could do was stand up and tell the honest truth about myself in the hope of awakening some of them to the deepening quagmire they were in. The single reason I was able to change so much was because God answered my cry for help, and I was then willing to follow him. Only God can break the chains that hold people who have indulged in wrongdoing, whether they be in prison or not.

The meeting went quite well, but the chance for discussion afterwards was cut short by lockup time for the lads. On our return to the gatehouse, we met a few officers who remembered me from years ago. They seemed amazed that I'd made it in life. We stood having a good conversation together until it was time to go.

Before leaving, Chris asked them, 'How bad was Jimmy in those days?'

After a brief chat they said, 'He was one of the top three worst we've ever had. We still talk about him now. But it's nice to see things have turned out well.'

During the drive home their assessment of my past behaviour rang in my ears. I knew I'd been bad, but not *that* bad. It made my salvation appear all the more powerful.

Chris and I made a number of visits to speak in various prisons together for a couple of years, although my availability was restricted by the demands of my job.

It was my involvement with Prison Fellowship that brought me into contact with a man who has since become a firm friend, Noel Fellowes. He was the main speaker at a dinner I'd been invited to attend in Liverpool.

His story was a harrowing one of injustice. He'd been interrogated, charged and convicted of a killing he knew nothing about. As an ex-policeman he was given hell by the prison population for the duration of his seven-year sentence. Only several years after he'd served his sentence was the real culprit discovered, but by then the damage to Noel had already been done. He remained imprisoned in bitterness, fear and complete emotional turmoil until one day he surrendered his life to God, which in turn brought a new freedom.

During his talk, Noel skated over a subject that convicted me that night—the issue of trust. He said that after the police, the courts, his barrister, the jury, the prison staff and the prisoners had utterly let him down, all trust had been broken. Noel went on to say that the only person he learnt to trust was himself. He relied on nobody else.

'That's me right now,' I thought as he spoke. 'I don't trust anybody at all.'

I had no idea where the roots of my mistrust lay, but the many years spent hopping between the streets and prison wouldn't have helped.

It was interesting to chat with Noel after the meeting. He was very interested in the work I did among the young people in the city. We exchanged phone numbers before parting and kept in touch. A few weeks after the dinner he came to visit our centre.

After five years of living in Paterson Street, with both our girls getting older, we decided it was time to buy a bigger house. Six eventful years had elapsed since I'd received the message to stay within these streets. Many times I'd wanted to run away but had held on by the skin of my teeth.

We didn't plan to move out of the area in which we knew God wanted us to stay, so we began searching for a bigger house in the neighbourhood. As we looked at various properties a pattern of messages came our way from a number of sources concerning faith and trust. We recognised the importance of making the right move and so we committed our endeavours to God in prayer each day.

It was during one of these times that a startling message popped through that challenged my whole way of thinking. It seemed to say:

'Why do you have to buy? Why not rent?'

This may seem innocuous enough, but at that time people who rented were looked on as idiots; buying was the big trend. We'd fallen into the same way of thinking ourselves, never considering anything other than using the profit from the sale of the first house to buy a bigger one.

Joanne and I discussed it at length and decided to rent a house if we found one that seemed appropriate.

Letting go of the compulsive urge to buy brought a new sense of lightness to our minds. A heaviness disappeared that had subconsciously been pulling us down. As our house sale drew closer without our having found somewhere else to live, God's voice came reaching through to me once again: 'I'll give you the choice, Jimmy —whether you worry or you don't worry!'

He was challenging me to relinquish my hold on all of our affairs and trust him. Many parts of the Bible passed through my mind that talked about God's loving provision for his people, his urge for them not to worry.

'OK, God,' I said. 'I'll do it. I hand it all over to you as from this moment.'

Joanne had been receiving strong messages at the same time about building God's kingdom. Many Bible passages we came across spoke of God's sadness at seeing his kingdom in ruins. Since I'd become a manager, we'd become more concerned with the things money could buy than with helping the poor or reaching out to the unsaved and encouraging struggling believers.

After pledging ourselves to let go of the distractions, we became available once more to those around us who needed help.

Shortly after this, we stumbled on a beautiful house that had all the space and facilities we needed. We'd found it without all our struggling and striving.

After tying up our affairs in Paterson Street, we were left with a profit from the sale amounting to a few thousand pounds. Instead of spending it, we prayed to God about what to do with it. He drew our attention to a group of people who worked hard doing good work but who were short of money. We donated it to them anonymously. The old Bible saying, 'It is more blessed to give than to receive,' proved true on this occasion as we benefited as much as those who received the cash.

The day before moving, I had to wait in the new house for the gas man to arrive and connect us to the supply. As I sat in a comfortable chair looking out through the patio doors into the back garden, fear swept over me like a wave.

A voice came nagging into my mind which tried to undermine the things we were seeking to do:

'What have you done? What's happened to all your security? You're a fool. Everybody'll realise how stupid you are when you fall on your face. If you lose your job, you'll also lose your house. Then your family'll have nothing. What kind of husband and father are you?'

Suddenly it seemed as if I'd gone completely in the wrong direction. I sat there feeling insecure, as if disaster was about to come my way.

'Did God *really* speak to me?' I asked myself. 'Or have I made this whole thing up?'

As I wrestled with these terrible thoughts, the memory of how real God had always been to me came steadily back to mind. He'd done so many irrefutable things in my life that I'd have to be kidding myself to deny his existence.

The source of the negative message was my enemy, the devil. He was up to his old tricks, trying to undermine the lives of Christians. A name Jesus used in describing Satan was 'Liar'. He goes around causing untold misery by twisting the truth.

I was still reeling from the knock this attack had given me. But I got out of my chair and began praying out loud in every room in the house until the doubts had been beaten right out of my system.

No doubt, Satan would be back another day, using another guise, employing another subtle tactic with which to bring me down. My struggle with him will go on until I reach the grave. But for now he was completely defeated.

Not long after moving to our new house, Joanne and I began receiving messages through our daily Bible readings about moving out into a new land. We'd always looked forward to the day when this phase of our life was finished in order to settle somewhere more permanently.

The same kind of feeling came over me as I walked along the dockside during lunch-hour at work one day. Both my grandfathers had worked in industries essential to the heartbeat of Liverpool. One of them built ships in Cammel Lairds shipyard all his working life, while the other spent his life sailing those same ships across the seven seas.

Such identity with the strength of the city—and the opportunity to contribute to its welfare through meaningful employment—was a privilege missing in the lives of many people in my generation. But as I looked at those historic docks on that sunny day I realised I'd touched base with the place itself. I'd worked hard and contributed much to the social needs of the day.

'I can leave this city now,' I said to myself. 'I've touched it's heart.'

13
Entering a new season

Having been a Christian for eight years, I became tired of beating a path from my past life into the jungle of the future.

I felt the need to exist in a place where I could simply be the new person I'd become—not an ex-con, ex-drunk, ex-fighter or ex- anything. It seemed impossible to gain a perspective about myself while still entrenched in the bustling environment that had spawned my wild behaviour as a boy.

These rumblings of discontent were similar to those of a teenager wanting to leave school or a student nearing the end of a long period of training.

'Is there a change in store, or is it just wishful thinking?' I asked myself. The only way to find out was to put one step in front of the other and see what the coming year held.

It began with a trip to the USA to visit my old friend, David Fox. Year after year I'd promised to travel over there, but I'd been afraid of being rejected by immigration owing to my criminal record. Visiting the USA with its different culture would serve as an ideal place from which to gain some perspective on my life.

During the two weeks before departure the name 'Joshua' kept springing to mind, though I couldn't understand why. In an effort to discover the meaning, I got hold of a tape called *Joshua Tree* by U2—a band widely known to be Christian—and listened to it throughout the trip.

Flying to New York was the fulfilment of a boyhood dream, a dream which for many years had appeared lost under thick clouds of imprisonment.

After passing through immigration, I caught an internal flight to Pittsburg, where I was met by David and his daughter, Joyce. Meeting him on his own soil was quite strange, a real departure from our years of communication which, for my part, had been centred around events in the streets back home.

We drove in his large comfortable vehicle, which was like a luxury minibus, through the darkness across the state line from Pennsylvania into Ohio and on to his home near Akron. Meeting David's wife, Fayne, was a real pleasure. We'd only ever spoken briefly on the telephone a few times—she was a lovely lady.

After supper I headed off to bed. But despite feeling exhausted after all the hours that had been added to my day, I could hardly sleep a wink, excitement still remaining inside.

The next morning, David and I got up early to attend the morning service at his church, called The Chapel, in Akron. Don't be fooled by the name 'Chapel' like I was; unlike the tiny British chapel, this place is a modern, multifunctional building which has over 8000 visitors each Sunday. Some chapel!

I was impressed with the spacious comfort in which proceedings took place. Nobody had to be squashed into a corner to do their bit. We sat with David's friend, Jack, who insisted on buying us breakfast at a nearby restaurant afterwards. We had good fun sitting, chatting together.

When we returned to the house, Fayne had a beautiful lunch prepared. I thus began the biggest pig-out I've ever had over two weeks in my life. American portions are *unbelievable!*

During the visit, we drove up to Buffalo to see Niagara Falls, which are magnificent, then across the border into Canada to visit Toronto. We stayed in a big hotel and met up with some of David's friends who worked way up north as missionaries with the American Indians.

As usual, we ate out at a restaurant, this time a pizza parlour. It was interesting to hear details of the work these men were involved in.

On the way back, we crossed the border further west to spend a day at the Ford Museum in Detroit. It was a fascinating place that displayed the history of American farm machinery, along with a whole series of classic cars produced in the USA over many years.

A more bizarre feature was the car in which President Kennedy had been shot dead in 1963. The traumatic newsreel I'd seen so many times now played once again across my mind. What a contrast to see this carrier of a piece of modern history sitting so quietly, almost forlorn! The story attached to it set it at odds with everything else in the museum.

Arriving back at David's place was a relief; the travelling had worn me out. Not being a touristy person I was quite content to spend my time in the local community or strolling in the grounds around the house. David's place was situated among the fruit trees David farmed each year, along with some woodland over to one side. Since my time in hospital, I'd fallen into the habit of quiet meditation. Quite often I mulled over a verse from the Bible for a long time while out walking among the trees.

A couple of days after our return, I sat having a long conversation with Fayne while David took a nap. As I explained the situation back home, an overwhelming urge came over me to read my Bible alone in my room. I'd learnt over the years not to ignore these promptings from within so excused myself from Fayne's company and went to my room.

Once inside, I sat on the bed, put the Bible on my knee and said to God: 'OK, here I am. What do you want me to read?'

Before the words were off my lips the name Joshua again came strongly into my mind.

'Are you *sure* about that?' I asked, not quite believing there could be anything of use inside that particular book to relate to my present situation. Once again the name Joshua flashed into mind. Turning to begin the book at the first chapter, my doubts were scattered when the verses began leaping off the page at me.

The whole tone of the message fitted perfectly with other pieces of the jigsaw of messages which, until now, had floated around without any firm basis. God was talking about moving out into a new land. He was saying that the time for it would be soon and that he'd be with me no matter where I went.

I tried to read on into chapter two, but it didn't feel right. The message had been delivered sharply in the first chapter. After a short time of prayer I emerged from my room to rejoin Fayne in the front room.

'I think I need to go out for a walk. God's spoken to me very strongly from the first chapter of Joshua. I'm not clear what it'll involve, but I need to walk it around the woods and sort it out in my mind.'

As I spoke, David came out from his room quietly to listen to the words I had to say. When I'd finished, he placed his hand on my shoulder.

'Fayne sent this Bible to me in 1942 while I was serving with the navy in the South Pacific during the war. She wrote a verse in the front which she believed God wanted me to hear. It's written here—have a look,' he said, passing the book across.

It was incredible. They were the very same words I'd read and then spoken to Fayne only moments before. A quietness surrounded the three of us as we realised God's presence in the situation. God had spoken in a very emphatic way.

I went outside for my walk but had only gone 30 yards when tears began to roll down my face. These gave way to great sobs as I walked slowly along. The implications behind the message dredged up many emotions. My time in Birkenhead on many occasions had been almost too hard to bear, taking me to the brink time and again, until I learnt to trust God and grasp the power in the name of his Son, Jesus.

This event happened during my second week in the USA, when I began missing Joanne and the girls terribly. It was the longest I'd spent away from them and it helped me realise afresh how much I loved them and, more importantly, how much I needed them.

Throughout my life I'd avoided needing anybody for fear of their letting me down. Any hint of disapproval from a person would result in my dropping him or her like a hot potato. Ever since we became engaged, I'd always wanted to trust myself to Joanne. But trying to reverse an ingrained trend doesn't happen overnight. It was worth going through the pain of separation for the sake of knowing that my heart was softening enough to allow people to mean something to me again.

My time with David finished on a much higher note than on our previous meeting. David, Fayne and Joyce all travelled to Pittsburg International Airport to see me off. On the way home, it was hard to believe I'd finally achieved my dream of visiting the USA. It certainly helped broaden my horizons considerably.

Back home, life carried on in a busy fashion; my job presented greater challenges, our marriage went from strength to strength and the girls were running around full of life.

Noel Fellowes continued to keep in touch, visiting the office several times. Eventually, he brought his wonderful wife, Coral, to stay with us. Noel and Coral were great company and seemed to operate on a higher spiritual plane than we did, which brought us to realise there was still much to learn.

Since the beginning of our Christian rebirth God had placed special people along our path to help us on the way. Noel and Coral were two more of those guiding lights. They spoke to us about the real need to be equipped by the infilling of the Holy Spirit. This would make us more effective in our own lives and help us deal with other spiritual matters.

During our Christian life Joanne and I had come across a number of people who operated in the gifts of the Holy Spirit, but we'd never felt directly challenged by it ourselves. My cautionary nature made me back off to think about what Noel and Coral had said, but before they left Joanne began to speak in tongues.

It was obvious that another challenge was on the horizon. I wondered whether I had the strength to overcome yet another hurdle after battling through so much over the years. During the weeks following Noel and Coral's visit, a frustration began to build up in me regarding my progress as a Christian. I'd heard many stories about people entering into a new spiritual understanding, but it seemed beyond my grasp.

I decided to write them a letter outlining many of the fears, attitudes, frustrations and general problems I had that I felt could be contributing to the blockage in my spiritual development. It was a measure of my confidence in them that I was able to share the secrets of my heart so openly in this way, though I had to get the letter to the mailbox quickly before I changed my mind!

Their response was encouraging. They phoned back right

away to assure me of their prayers and support, and they arranged to visit us again within two weeks.

Sometimes in life we walk around the edge of a situation for a long time before making the leap—a split second after jumping, we know there's no going back. The situation I'd put myself into with Noel and Coral was like this. I'd made the jump and now awaited the splash.

The day of their visit soon came round. It was great to see them again as we'd become very fond of them as a couple. After putting the children to bed, we settled ourselves comfortably in the front room before embarking on what turned out to be an epic struggle.

In a cautionary manner, Coral asked if she could share with me the things God had revealed to her when she'd been praying for me during the previous few weeks. With my agreement she told me of five things God had revealed. They almost blew my head off! Coral had hit the nail on the head five times. It's a very uncomfortable feeling sitting there having somebody expose things from deep within, things that humanly speaking she could never have known.

Shortly after these revelations we started to pray. Noel and Coral began receiving fractured pictures of incidents from my past that had left indelible marks on my personality. Much of what came to the surface was endemic of the wild mentality I'd adopted as a boy, a mentality that now had to be rooted out.

Having spent so many years trying to sort myself out, I found it a great disappointment to discover all this junk under the crust of my *persona*. Many of these bad things had taken on spiritual identities that clung to the walls of my life, crippling my progress as a Christian.

Having clearly identified things from which I needed to be set free, Noel, Coral and Joanne began cutting me off from them in Jesus' name. I kept on expecting a flash of light or Jesus to walk into the room to confirm the reality of what was going on. Nothing inside seemed to stir me at all.

There were things I needed to repent of, too, habits I'd dragged into my Christian life that were unacceptable. Confession and repentance to God is the only way in which a person can truly be set free from the wrong they've indulged in.

This was deep spiritual surgery, cutting into the real me. I had to own it and wear it. The battle was on.

Noel stood holding my hands, battling in prayer against a presence in me that symbolised all I'd been in the past, a character with massive proportions who wanted to stay. As Noel identified this character, he asked me to renounce it. But I found that too difficult. It'd be like throwing a part of myself away. The intensity of the struggle had Noel shaking from head to foot.

As I stood there undecided, I was reminded of the drug addict who succumbs to the demon drug and the alcoholic who gives in to the desire for liquor. In those moments my struggle was similar. My weakness and inability were pathetic, but somehow from somewhere deep inside I mustered enough determination to renounce this thing outright.

No sooner had the words left my lips than Noel was restored to peace. Letting go of my hands, he returned to slump wearily back into his chair. We all felt exhausted after having been at it for two hours, and a deep sense of victory prevailed as we sat around talking. But I wondered if it had all been real. I didn't seem any different now than before we'd started.

'Am I just kidding myself?' I thought.

After a few minutes I voiced my fears. 'I know what we've been through's incredible. I really appreciate everything you've done, but I don't really feel any different. It's as if I need a sign to confirm that what's happened has been for real.'

Coral answered first, a look of bemusement on her face.

'Jimmy, I don't know how you can say that after God revealed to us so many things we couldn't have known. Aren't they a sign to you?'

'Yes, I suppose they are,' I said. But I still felt uncertain.

After a few moments I spoke again. 'Look I don't want to sound as if I doubt the reality of what God's done, but I think I need something tangible to hold on to.'

Noel, who'd been sitting quietly, listening intently, suddenly spoke up. 'I know what it is,' he said, rising. 'Come here, Jim.'

As I stood before him, once more he took my hands in his. He said, 'While I pray, I want you to keep repeating that word you told us about earlier.'

The word was one that kept coming into my head while I was walking around the grounds of David Fox's farm in the USA. It sounded like an Indian name.

I did as Noel asked without questioning why. Then, after a few moments, my head began to tingle with a buzz like having gas at the dentist. Everything seemed far away. Noel's voice sounded distant, my limbs went loose, then my mouth began to speak rapidly with unintelligible words.

'I don't believe it,' I thought to myself. 'I'm speaking in tongues!'

The four of us stood praising God in tongues for a few minutes before breaking into laughter together. This was the seal I'd been looking for, the sign that confirmed all God had delivered me from on this night. The Bible makes it clear that when rubbish is cleared out of a person it must be replaced by God's Holy Spirit, otherwise the person could end up in an even worse mess. My speaking in tongues was a sign to me that the Holy Spirit had entered into all the areas in my life previously filled with undesirable things.

Alongside other breakthroughs over the years this particular development was of immense significance, enabling me to operate in a more effective manner from then on.

The closing chapter of my time within these streets came as a result of Noel inviting me to speak at a seminar in the Midlands a few weeks later. When he phoned to say the meeting was on a Monday afternoon, I almost laughed. The demands of my job kept my diary crammed to bursting-point week after week.

'I really believe God wants you to come, Jimmy. What do you think?'

It didn't make any sense in terms of my time schedule, but something told me I should go along.

'Noel, I'm too busy to go, especially on a weekday, but something inside tells me you're right. You book me in and I'll juggle my diary and be there.'

This wasn't the first time I'd been drawn into a situation without understanding why. The meaning often became more apparent at a later date. The venue was a holiday conference centre filled with thousands of Christians who attended a wide variety of seminars and lectures throughout each day. My job would be to speak alongside Noel and his colleague from Prison Fellowship, Peter Chadwick, about the ministry of Prison Fellowship.

I arrived in time for lunch and enjoyed polishing off the last of Noel's favourite fruit loaf for dessert, much to his dismay!

The seminar itself went very smoothly. Each of us spoke clearly to the well-attended assembly before fielding questions from the floor. Many people pledged their support for the work of Prison Fellowship.

However, nothing particularly outstanding took place as far as I was concerned. Maybe I'd been kidding myself about this visit. Nevertheless, it was good to be with Noel and Coral again.

In the evenings the 8000 or so people on camp had the opportunity to come together for a big celebration meeting, including a sermon from a frontline speaker. I half considered heading for home after supper—a busy day awaited me at the office in the morning—but such was Noel's enthusiasm that I allowed myself to be persuaded.

As we sat in the vast hall waiting for things to start, my mind was filled with how late it would be after the long drive home and how tired I'd be in the morning. But my idle concerns were soon put to flight by the worship, which broke out as the band began to play.

It's an utterly incredible experience to be among thousands of people who sing together their praises to our God, the King. It's like being transported into paradise. We sang song after song, the vast sea of voices rising and falling like great waves on the ocean. I could have carried on all night. But after the band had done their job correctly in leading us into God's presence with praise, they eventually brought their session to a close.

Next on to the platform was our main speaker, a man named Larry Tomczak from the USA, who spoke with great authority, holding everybody's attention immediately. He certainly grabbed my attention when he announced the theme of his message: 'Entering a New Season'.

He then began to unpack all the Bible passages that had taken on strong significance to Joanne and me over the past few months. Each of them spoke about moving out into a new land. All the hints and signs indicating our time in Birkenhead was coming to an end were emphatically confirmed by everything Larry said. It was as if he were speaking to me alone, such was the accuracy of his words.

Noel leant forward and smiled at me along the row as he knew what was happening. Sometimes extraordinary things happen that, far from our taking hold of them, we find them floating over our heads. That sensation happened to me. Larry brought me sailing back down to earth during his summing up. He spoke of a time 10 years before when, after beginning to feel unsettled in his circumstances, he'd decided to take some time out with his family. The city to which they withdrew was Cleveland in the USA.

I could hardly believe my ears. Only a few months ago I'd withdrawn for the same reasons to the same country and spent time in Cleveland myself! I sat there completely stunned. It was as if God was slapping me over the head with messages to say, 'Wakey, wakey, Jimmy Rice. I'm speaking to you, yes, *you*! Are you going to listen this time?'

After the meeting we sat drinking coffee in a cafe adjoining the meeting hall, discussing what a great meeting it had been. I was unable to stay for long owing to the long drive facing me, so I said my goodbyes and hit the road. As I sped along homeward, the years I'd spent within those streets began flooding back through my mind. I could hardly believe they were coming to an end.

Those streets had been my college of life, a place where I'd learnt to stop running and face up to myself. I'd been broken and fashioned into the person God wanted me to be, yet had ample opportunity to reject him if I'd wanted to. As a man who sought truth and reality, I could no more deny the hand that saved and rebuilt me than the mother who bore me, nor exchange what I knew to be the truth for a life of lies.

Within a year of receiving Larry's message, we'd moved on to pastures new, but not before Joanne had given birth to our third daughter, Ruby Joy.

I finish with the words that best describe my life. They were written by King David of Israel in Psalm 40 (Living Bible):

'I waited patiently for God to help me; then he listened and heard my cry. He lifted me out of the pit of despair, out from the bog and the mire, and set my feet on a hard, firm path and steadied me as I walked along. He has given me a new song to sing, of praises to our God. Now many will hear of the glorious things he did for me, and stand in awe before the Lord, and put their trust in him.'

If God can do it for me, he can surely do it for you!

Acknowledgements

Words can't adequately express the extent to which I appreciate those among my family and friends who refused to give up on me and helped me make it. There are too many names to mention here, but you all know who you are.

A special thank you to Annette for her willingness to type and retype the manuscript, sometimes into the early hours of the morning.

If after reading this book you'd like further help, please contact your prison chaplain or write to Jimmy Rice at:

Prison Book Ministries Ltd
PO Box 40
Hinckley
Leicestershire LE10 3LX
UK

Prison Book Ministries Ltd works in partnership in the UK with Prison Fellowship, a national organisation which currently has over 150 voluntary support groups. These offer practical help, love, support and care to prisoners, ex-prisoners and their families.

We're here to help you!

Издательство "Протестант", отпечатано с готовых диапозитивов в полиграфической фирме "Красный пролетарий". Заказ №3864.